thank you notes

thank you

40 Handmade Ways to Show You're Grateful

notes

Jan Stephenson Kelly & Amy Appleyard

 **LARK BOOKS**

A Division of Sterling Publishing Co., Inc.

New York / London

Editors: Brian Sawyer and Kathleen McCafferty
Managing Editors: Aimee Chase and Rebecca Springer
Art Director: Wendy Simard
Managing Art Director: Shannon Yokeley
Photographer: Allan Penn
Photography: Rebecca Springer
Cover and Interior Designer: woolypear

Library of Congress Cataloging-in-Publication Data

Stephenson, Jan.
  Thank you notes : 40 handmade ways to show you're grateful / Jan
Stephenson & Amy Appleyard. -- 1st ed.
      p. cm.
  Includes index.
  ISBN 978-1-60059-469-4 (pb-pbk.)
  1. Greeting cards. 2. Thank-you notes. I. Appleyard, Amy. II. Title.
  TT872.S825 2009
  745.594'1--dc22

                          2008054389

10 9 8 7 6 5 4 3 2 1

First Edition

Published by Lark Books, A Division of
Sterling Publishing Co., Inc.
387 Park Avenue South, New York, NY 10016

© 2009, Lark Books, a Division of Sterling Publishing Co., Inc.

Distributed in Canada by Sterling Publishing,
c/o Canadian Manda Group, 165 Dufferin Street
Toronto, Ontario, Canada M6K 3H6

Distributed in the United Kingdom by GMC Distribution Services,
Castle Place, 166 High Street, Lewes, East Sussex, England BN7 1XU

Distributed in Australia by Capricorn Link (Australia) Pty Ltd.,
P.O. Box 704, Windsor, NSW 2756 Australia

The written instructions, photographs, designs, patterns, and projects in this
volume are intended for the personal use of the reader and may be reproduced
for that purpose only. Any other use, especially commercial use, is forbidden
under law without written permission of the copyright holder.

Every effort has been made to ensure that all the information in this book is
accurate. However, due to differing conditions, tools, and individual skills, the
publisher cannot be responsible for any injuries, losses, and other damages
that may result from the use of the information in this book.

If you have questions or comments about this book, please contact:
Lark Books
67 Broadway
Asheville, NC 28801
828-253-0467

Manufactured in China

ISBN 13: 978-1-60059-319-2

For information about custom editions, special sales, premium and corporate
purchases, please contact Sterling Special Sales Department at 800-805-5489
or specialsales@sterlingpub.com.

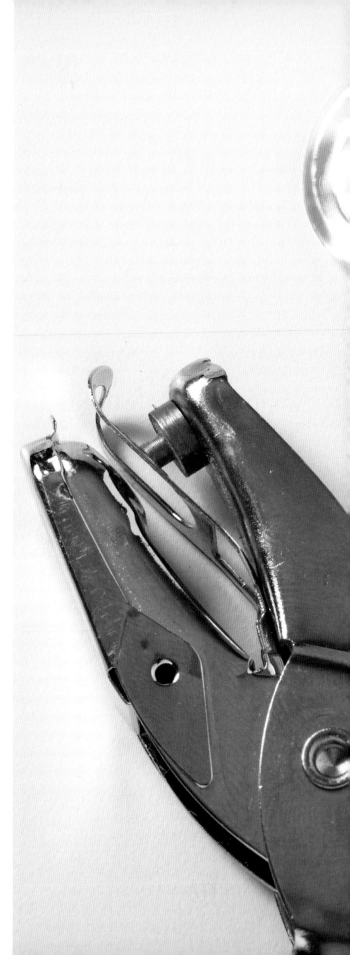

To all who create
beauty in this world,
be they crafty or not.

thank you for your time

Contents

Introduction

We all feel it at some point—the chore that can be a thank you note. As children, our mothers (or teachers) taught us the *necessity* of writing a thank you note. And so this communiqué has earned a bad reputation for bestowing guilt upon us during the otherwise happy experience of receiving a gift.

But here is the secret, the silver lining. The thank you note can actually be our *friend*. When created with care and love, it can be a joy for the sender as well as the recipient. Sure, writing thank you notes is a valuable life skill. This simple act places us among those with manners, those who are cultured. But it is also a rare opportunity in our hectic lives to pause for a few minutes and give thanks.

There are many good reasons for sending a thank you note. We generally do it to show our gratitude for a gift received for a special occasion such as a wedding, birthday, graduation, anniversary, or upon the arrival of a new baby. Whether the gift is useful or simply beautiful, a note of thanks signals our appreciation for the object as well as the thoughtfulness, time, and energy that went into the act of gift-giving. If a gift is received by mail, a thank you note also serves the practical purpose of letting the giver know that we have received their gift.

There are more subtle gifts that also warrant a note of thanks. A friend may show us kindness with encouraging or sympathetic words during a challenging time. A colleague might notice something they can do to make our lives a little easier. Or, a friend opens their home to us for a meal or an overnight visit. These are all wonderful reasons to send a thank you note.

Being grateful is extremely good for us. The simple act of writing a thank you note—of acknowledging our gratefulness for something, no matter how small—can have a healing effect. It keeps us focused on the good in the world. And at the end of a long day, sitting down to create a handmade thank you note can open us up to positive feelings about our family, our friends, and our lives.

This book will detail all the tools, materials, and techniques you need to create a variety of beautiful handmade cards to thank the most important people in your life. Handmade thank you notes are appropriate for anyone—thus, many of the cards you will discover in this book were designed with children, parents, siblings, friends, and other important relations in mind. Imagine how appreciative they will be, knowing that you spent your time and effort thinking of how to show your gratitude in a special way. That's a rarity in this fast-paced, e-mail-savvy world.

Whether you are a new or seasoned paper crafter, feel free to use this book as a source of inspiration as well as a reference guide. You get to choose the style, greeting, and message—be it humorous, heartfelt, or romantic. One of the best things about giving a handmade card is that you can add your own personal touch. You may replicate the cards featured in these pages, or simply use these examples as a jumping-off point for your own creativity. Read the book from start to finish, or refer to the guides and samples from time to time to encourage fresh ideas.

Chapter 1 provides a pictorial overview of the various tools and materials used to complete the cards highlighted in this book. Bring this book with you to your local craft store and use it as a resource to quickly and easily identify the products you will need. Chapter 2 focuses on thank you notes geared to specific people such as mom, dad, sister, and teacher. Chapter 3 highlights thank you notes appropriate for acknowledging gifts such as flowers, money, kindness, sharing a special day, sympathy, and more. Chapters 4 features handmade cards focused on lovers—husbands, wives, boyfriends, or girlfriends. Chapter 5 provides "just because" cards—useful for everyday notes of thanks. Of course, any of the designs featured in this book can be adapted to suit the recipient of your card with just a few simple language adjustments.

No matter how intricate the card design, the most important ingredient in a thank you note is a sincere message. Turn to the section on Expressions of Thanks for thoughts on how to compose your own greetings or find quotations to adorn your handmade cards. It also explores the basic components of writing a thoughtful, personalized message to capture your emotions and shows ways to incorporate handwritten elements, even for those who dislike their own handwriting. As always, it's the thought that counts.

We hope *Thank You Notes* will encourage and guide you through the process of creating handmade cards, a considerate gesture that shows genuine appreciation.

CHAPTER 1

Materials and Tools

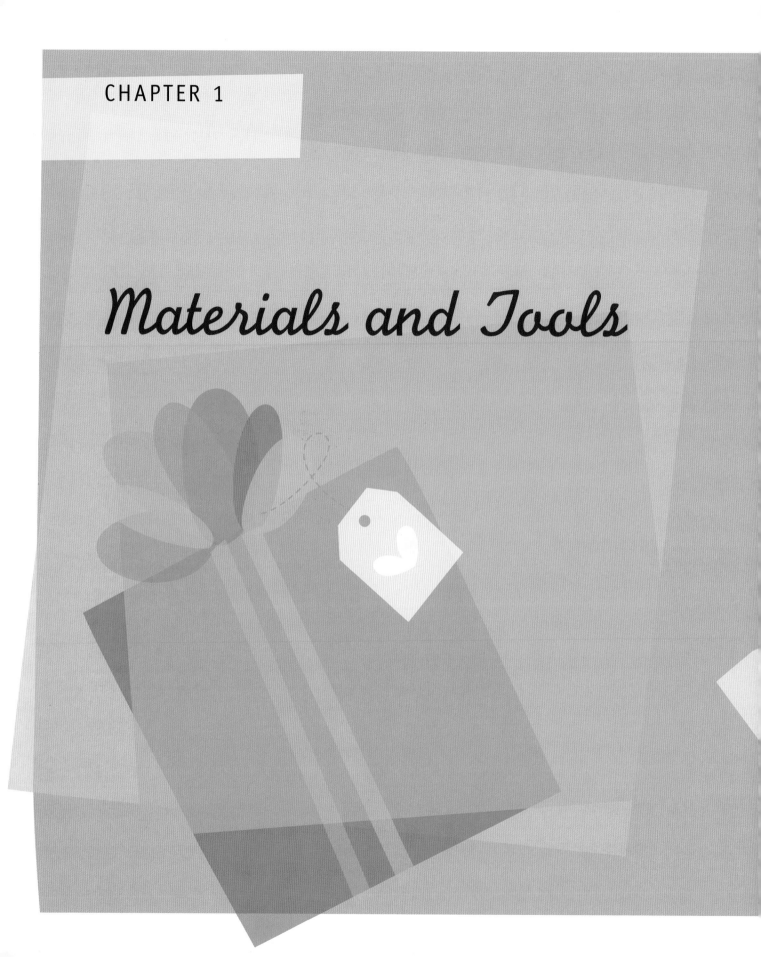

The handmade cards featured in *Thank You Notes* were created using a variety of tools and materials that can be found at your local craft store. Refer to the supply list for each card before shopping for tools and materials to create your cards. In some cases, you may find you have exactly what you need in your craft stash at home. Of course, you can always create a variation of any of the designs in this book by using what you have, or by trying something new. The key is to be creative—and have fun!

MATERIALS

Cardstock and Note Cards

Heavy-weight cardstock or premade blank note cards serve as the base for handmade cards.

Paper and Paper Substitutes

Solid and patterned paper, vellum, metallic paper, clear plastic, fabric, leather, and other paper substitutes add texture and graphic design elements.

Envelopes and Templates

Use white or colored store-bought envelopes in sizes A2, A4, or square, or create your own envelopes using envelope templates.

Adhesives

Liquid glue, glue pens, double-sided tape, tape runners, glue dots, glitter glue, spray adhesive, Fabric-Tac, and foam mounting squares are common adhesives.

Writing and Coloring Instruments

Keep a variety of pencils, journaling pens, colored markers, glitter pens, gel markers, foam markers, and other writing instruments on hand.

Stamps and Ink

Rubber, foam, and acrylic stamps provide images, sentiments, and details you can use on cards again and again. Invest in an array of ink pads, stamping markers, and acrylic paints to color stamped images.

Ribbon and Trimmings

Ribbon, twine, embroidery floss, thread, yarn, and craft wire can add a creative flourish to cards.

Stickers and Rub-ons

Stickers and rub-on transfers come in a variety of colors, sizes, styles, and materials, and are perfect for adding words, phrases, or design elements to cards.

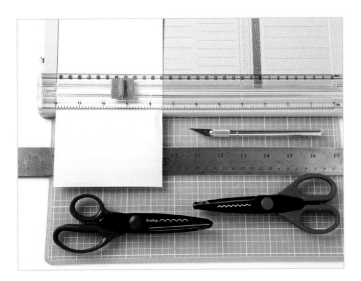

Attachments and Embellishments

Get creative with brads, eyelets, metal-rimmed tags, glitter, staples, safety pins, beads, chipboard (decorated cardboard), and other card accents.

TOOLS

Paper Trimmers

Measure and cut cardstock, paper, and photos with a paper trimmer or use a cutting mat, a ruler, and a craft knife.

Hole Punchers

Use an awl to make small punctures in cardstock or paper for hand sewing. Hole punches in sizes $\frac{1}{16}$, $\frac{1}{8}$, and $\frac{1}{4}$ inch are commonly used for punching holes for brads and eyelets.

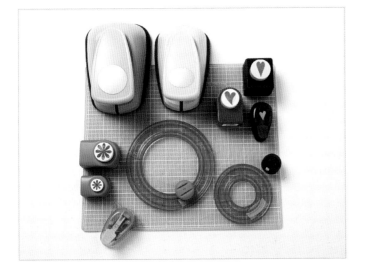

Eyelet-setting Tools

Invest in an all-in-one universal hole punch/eyelet setter, or use a small hammer, a hole punch, and an eyelet setter.

Scissors

Use regular scissors to cut cardstock and paper, and decorative-edged scissors to make scalloped edges and more.

Bone Folder

A bone folder adds a professional-looking crease to score (fold) cardstock into a card base.

Sewing Machine

Quickly and easily add zigzag- or straight-stitch elements to your cards by machine sewing on paper.

Computer and Printer

Create card greetings and messages with word-processing software, fonts, and a color inkjet printer.

Cutting Systems and Punches

Cutting systems and handheld punches can be used to cut letters, numbers, and shapes, or to round or design card corners.

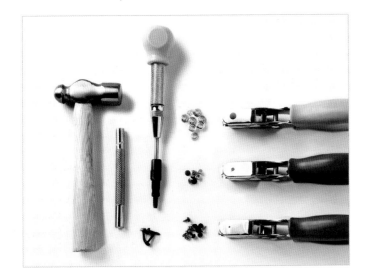

CHAPTER 2

Thanks to You! Cards

We all know it is the people in our lives that make life sweet. When they honor us with a thoughtful present or a gift of their time and energy, we can return the favor by thanking them with a handmade card that is also an expression of how special they are to us. There are many opportunities to celebrate those around you for their generosity. Mothers, fathers, grandparents, siblings, teachers, husbands, wives, lovers, friends, and even coworkers will all delight in a handmade card that is a true expression of your gratitude.

Great Teacher

by CANDICE CRUZ

*Create this fun tag card for your child's favorite teacher
or someone who has taught you something new.*

SUPPLIES

Tools

- ☐ paper trimmer or cutting mat, craft knife, and ruler
- ☐ bone folder
- ☐ popsicle stick

Materials

- ☐ white cardstock
- ☐ blue and brown striped paper
- ☐ spiral-bound notebook paper
- ☐ adhesive
- ☐ sandpaper
- ☐ six blue flowers

- ☐ mini glue dots
- ☐ 10 inches (25.4 cm) of green gros-grain ribbon, ⅜ inch (9.5 mm) wide
- ☐ six green brads, ⅜ inch (10 mm) diameter
- ☐ small alphabet rub-ons or stickers

INSTRUCTIONS

1. Cut the white cardstock to 8 inches tall x 9¼ inches wide (20.3 x 23.5 cm). Trim a piece of blue and brown striped paper to 1½ inches tall x 9¼ inches wide (3.8 x 23.5 cm). Cut the spiral-bound notebook paper to 3½ inches tall x 9¼ inches wide (8.9 x 23.5 cm).

2. Use the bone folder to score and fold white cardstock to form a 4-inch-tall x 9¼-inch-wide (10.2 x 23.5 cm) card base. Adhere blue and brown striped paper to the bottom of the front of the card. Adhere notebook paper to the top of the front of the card, overlapping the patterned paper.

TIP: Card opens from the bottom.

3. Using sandpaper, gently sand the edges of each flower to expose some of the inner core. Be gentle to avoid ripping off a petal. Adhere flowers to the card using mini glue dots.

4. Adhere the green ribbon to the card using mini glue dots. Glue the ribbon about ¼ inch (6 mm) above the torn edge of the notebook paper. Trim the ribbon edges flush with the edges of the card.

5. Cut the prongs off each brad and attach to the center of the flowers using a pop-up glue dot. Transfer rub-on letters spelling "thanks" with the popsicle stick so that each letter of the word goes onto its own brad.

6. Transfer letters spelling "for being a great teacher" onto the ribbon. Start from the right side to ensure the phrase is right justified. Adhere flowers to the front of the card above the ribbon.

Hey, Sis!

by CANDICE CRUZ

Show your sister how much you care with a card created in glittery pink cardstock and twinkle stickers.

SUPPLIES

Tools

- [ ] paper trimmer or cutting mat, craft knife, and ruler
- [ ] bone folder
- [ ] computer with word processing software and printer
- [ ] scissors

Materials

- [ ] shiny pink cardstock
- [ ] floral patterned paper
- [ ] 20 inches (50.8 cm) of white rick-rack trim, ½ inch (1.3 cm) wide
- [ ] mini glue dots
- [ ] liquid adhesive
- [ ] pink chipboard letters
- [ ] pink twinkle stickers
- [ ] white cardstock

INSTRUCTIONS

1. Cut the shiny pink cardstock to 8 inches tall x 9¼ inches wide (20.3 x 23.5 cm). Cut one piece of patterned paper to 3 inches tall x 9¼ inches wide (7.6 x 23.5 cm). Trim a second piece of patterned paper to 1¼ inches tall x 6¼ inches wide (3.2 x 15.9 cm). Cut white rickrack into two 10-inch (25.4 cm) lengths.

2. Score and fold the pink cardstock with the bone folder to create a 4-inch-tall x 9¼-inch-wide (10.2 x 23.5 cm) card base (card opens from bottom). Center and adhere the larger piece of patterned paper to the front of the card. Adhere the white rickrack along the edges of the floral paper with mini glue dots. The middle of the rickrack should cover the edges of the patterned paper. Trim off any excess rickrack.

3. Adhere chipboard letters and punctuation marks to the front of the card, spelling "Hey, Sis!" Start with the exclamation point and work backwards. Adhere the pink twinkle stickers to the chipboard letters.

4. Using a computer with word processing software, write "I am grateful for you!" and print the sentiment onto white cardstock. Cut the phrase to 1 inch tall x 6 inches wide (2.5 x 15.2 cm), leaving 1 inch (2.5 cm) of space on each side of the phrase. Mount the cut phrase onto the smaller piece of patterned paper. Center and adhere it to the inside of the card, then adhere three pink twinkle stickers to each side of the phrase.

Better Half

by KELLY PURKEY

Celebrate a lover or even a friend who is your "better half" with this unique, number-shaped card.

INSTRUCTIONS

1. Draw the number "1" onto a piece of patterned paper and the number "2" onto a different style of patterned paper with a pencil and cut them out using scissors. Finished size of numbers should be 2½ inches tall x 1½ inches wide (6.4 x 3.8 cm). Draw and cut out a slash from a third type of patterned paper so that the finished size is 4¾ inches tall x ¾ inch wide (12.1 x 1.9 cm).

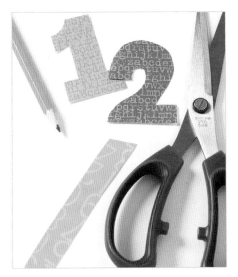

2. Cut a 9½-inch-tall x 3½-inch-wide (24.1 x 8.9 cm) piece of white cardstock. Use the bone folder to score and fold the card in half (card opens from the bottom). Lay the card flat, and adhere the "1," slash, and "2" to the front of the white cardstock, making sure the "1" and slash line up with the folded top edge of the white cardstock. Cut around the shapes, leaving the top fold intact.

3. Hand-sew two colored buttons to the "1," three different colored buttons to the slash, and two different buttons to the "2."

4. Use the popsicle stick to transfer black "thanks to my better half*" rub-ons onto the card.

Thanks, Dad

by KIM KESTI

Tell Dad just how grateful you are for his encouragement, financial support, or help.

SUPPLIES

Tools

- [ ] paper trimmer or cutting mat, craft knife, and ruler
- [ ] bone folder

Materials

- [ ] gray cardstock
- [ ] striped patterned paper
- [ ] circles transparency paper
- [ ] liquid adhesive
- [ ] one piece of gray felt, 1½ x 4½ inches (3.8 x 11.4 cm)
- [ ] circles embellishment
- [ ] small stitched leather frame
- [ ] retro black-and-white square tile alphabet letters

INSTRUCTIONS

1. Trim the gray cardstock to 6 inches tall x 7 inches wide (15.2 x 17.8 cm). Cut a strip of striped patterned paper to 2 inches tall x 6 inches wide (5 x 15.2 cm), making sure the stripes are vertical. Cut the circles transparency paper to 2 inches tall x 3 inches wide (5 x 7.6 cm).

2. Use the bone folder to score and fold gray cardstock in half to form a card base 3 inches tall x 7 inches wide (7.6 x 17.8 cm). Adhere the cut striped paper to the front of the card, leaving approximately ½ inch (1.3 cm) at the bottom of the card base.

3. Round the right edge of the gray felt piece. Center and adhere the circle embellishment in the rounded area. Glue the felt piece to the right side of the patterned paper strip on the front of the card. The rounded edge should hang off the card. Mount the cut circles transparency paper in the leather frame and adhere it on top of the felt piece.

4. Layer black-and-white square alphabet letters on the face of the frame to spell "Thanks Dad."

Merci Bucket

by RENÉE DeBLOIS

SUPPLIES

Tools

☐ small foam brush

☐ 1-inch (2.5 cm) scallop circle punch

☐ scissors

☐ pencil

☐ ruler

☐ large sticker-making machine

☐ fine-point black marker

Materials

☐ lime green acrylic paint

☐ lowercase white alphabet stickers, 2 inches (5 cm) square

☐ lime green glitter

☐ paint can (gallon-sized)

☐ pumpkin cardstock

☐ two photos, 8 inches tall x 10 inches wide (20.3 x 25.4 cm)

☐ 21 inches (53.3 cm) of circle patterned ribbon, ⅝ inch (1.6 cm) wide

☐ 12 inches (30.5 cm) of two different coordinating ribbons, ⅝ inch (1.6 cm) wide

☐ 18 pieces of coordinating ribbon and scrap fabric of various widths cut into 6-inch (15.2 cm) lengths

☐ silver belt buckle

"Merci beaucoup" becomes a "merci bucket" with this fanciful interpretation of a traditional greeting card, sure to delight its recipient with the goodies inside.

INSTRUCTIONS

1. Lightly coat the white letter stickers with lime green acrylic paint using the foam brush. Quickly coat the letters with lime green glitter and set them aside to dry overnight.

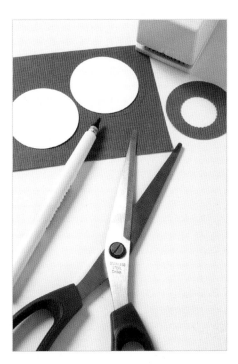

2. Trace the circle templates onto pumpkin cardstock and cut out two circles. Using the 1-inch (2.5 cm) scallop circle punch, punch out centers of circles.

3. Cut the front and back photos to 7⅜ inches tall x 10½ inches wide (18.7 x 26.7 cm). On each side, mark with a pencil 1½ inches (3.8 cm) from the top. Center a 1-inch (2.5 cm) circle punch over the marking and punch out half-circle notches to accommodate the paint can handles.

TIP: Template may be wider than your photos, which is fine because photo seams will be covered with ribbon.

4. Place the glittered alphabet stickers on the front-facing photo to spell out "merci" and "mom," using a ruler to guide your placement. Start with the letter "i," as this will be your tallest letter. Place all letters as close to the top and bottom of the photos as possible.

5. Feed photos (image side up), three longer pieces of ribbon, and the cardstock circles through the sticker-making machine. Detach the stickers from the machine and peel the clear film off each item.

TIP: If you don't have access to a sticker-making machine, you can print photos directly onto adhesive photo paper, which would make this step unnecessary for the photos but require adhesive for the ribbon and cardstock circles.

6. Adhere photos to the paint can. Start by fitting the half-circle notch cut out of the photo where the paint can handle is located. Your two photos will overlap at the sides.

8. Feed the other 12-inch-long (30.5 cm) ribbon through the silver buckle. Adhere the ribbon "belt" to the center of the paint can, overlapping ribbon at the ends. Tie the shorter ribbon to each handle and trim the ends. Fill the bucket with goodies.

7. Cut one of the 12-inch-long (30.5 cm) pieces of ribbon into four pieces: two 1-inch-long (2.5 cm) pieces and two 5-inch-long (12.7 cm) pieces. Attach the ribbon to the photo seams, skipping over the handle notches. Cut a slit at the radius of each orange cardstock circle. Adhere cardstock circles around the paint can handle notches.

Teacher Tags

by KIM KESTI

Use teacher-inspired details such as ruler accent ribbon to create this distinctive tag card.

SUPPLIES

Tools

☐ paper trimmer or cutting mat, craft knife, and ruler

☐ pinking shears

Materials

☐ ledger patterned paper

☐ phone book patterned paper

☐ red dots patterned paper

☐ small "thank you" tag embellishment

☐ red cardstock

☐ liquid adhesive

☐ black chipboard letters

☐ large kraft tag, 3⅛ inch tall x 6¼ inch wide (7.9 x 15.9 cm)

☐ medium manila tag, 2⅜ inch tall x 4¼ inch wide (6 x 10.8 cm)

☐ red library ring

☐ 6 inches (15.2 cm) of striped ribbon, ½ inch (1.3 cm) wide

☐ 6 inches (15.2 cm) of ruler ribbon, ½ inch (1.3 cm) wide

INSTRUCTIONS

1. Cut the ledger patterned paper to 3 inches tall x 5 inches wide (7.6 x 12.7 cm). Trim the phone book paper to 3 inches tall x 3 inches wide (7.6 x 7.6 cm). Cut the red dots paper to 3 inches tall x 1 inch wide (7.6 x 2.5 cm). Layer and adhere the pieces onto the large manila tag with the ledger on the bottom and the phone book and red dots on top.

2. Mat the small "thank you" tag embellishment with red cardstock, leaving a ¼-inch (6 mm) border around the edges of the tag. Trim the edges with pinking shears.

3. Adhere the chipboard letters to the "thank you" tag, spelling "Teacher." Adhere the "thank you" tag to the medium manila-colored tag.

4. Link the two finished tags together with library ring. Tie two 6-inch-long (15.2 cm) pieces of ribbon to the ring.

Baby Thanks

by CANDICE CRUZ

Send a thank you note as special as the baby gift they sent you.

SUPPLIES

Tools

- ☐ paper trimmer or cutting mat, craft knife, and ruler
- ☐ 2-inch (5 cm) circle cutting tool
- ☐ 3-inch (7.6 cm) scallop circle punch
- ☐ bone folder
- ☐ corner rounder

Materials

- ☐ white cardstock
- ☐ mustard cardstock
- ☐ green cardstock with rickrack border, 4¼ inches tall x 5½ inches wide (10.8 x 14 cm)
- ☐ 11 inches (27.9 cm) of peach ribbon, ¼ inch (6 mm) wide
- ☐ tape
- ☐ mini glue dots
- ☐ two ½-inch (1.3 cm) round orange buttons
- ☐ foam tape

INSTRUCTIONS

1. Cut the white cardstock to 8½ inches tall x 5¼ inches wide (21.6 x 13.3 cm). Cut a 2-inch (5 cm) circle out of mustard cardstock using the circle-cutting tool. Punch a 3-inch (7.6 cm) scalloped circle out of white cardstock with the scallop punch.

2. Use the bone folder to score and fold the white cardstock to create a 4¼-inch-tall x 5½-inch-wide (10.8 x 14 cm) card base. Center and adhere the green cardstock with rickrack border onto the front of the card.

TIP: Card opens from the bottom.

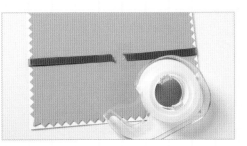

3. Wrap the peach ribbon around the middle of the card and tape the ends down on the front of the card.

4. Cut the mustard cardstock circle in half with the scissors. Then, cut one of the halves in half again to create a pie-shaped wedge. Center and adhere the bottom half of the circle to the bottom of the scalloped circle. Adhere one of the pie-shaped wedges to the top left to create the baby carriage, leaving a small gap between the pie-shaped wedge and the bottom half-circle.

5. Adhere the two orange buttons to the carriage with mini glue dots to create wheels. Adhere the finished scalloped circle piece to the center of the card using foam tape.

6. With word processing software, write "Thank you for the baby gift!" Print the message onto mustard cardstock. Cut the cardstock to 3¾ inches tall x 5 inches wide (9.5 x 12.7 cm). Round the corners using the corner rounder. Adhere the message to the inside of the card.

CHAPTER 3

Thank You For . . .

Cards

There are many ways people show us that they care with their gifts. They may give us some of their time to teach us something new or help us with a particular task. They show us compassion by listening to us and sharing in our experiences, whether in happiness or grief. Or they go to bat for us on an issue that is important. Sometimes, we want to showcase our gratefulness to a friend who shared a special day or event with us. And then there are the tangible gifts: money, flowers, or a special present to mark an occasion. Whether it is deliberate or a random act of kindness, an act of generosity by a family member, friend, or coworker can spark our gratitude and move us to create a handmade testimonial to our thanks.

Your Time

by CANDICE CRUZ

SUPPLIES

Tools

- ☐ 1/16-inch (1.5 mm) hole punch
- ☐ 1/8-inch (3 mm) hole punch
- ☐ 1/4-inch (6 mm) hole punch
- ☐ computer with word processing software and printer
- ☐ paper trimmer or cutting mat, craft knife, and ruler

Materials

- ☐ brown circle card, 5½ inch (14 cm) diameter
- ☐ mini glue dots
- ☐ large flower embellishment
- ☐ clock transparency
- ☐ white cardstock
- ☐ peach paper
- ☐ liquid adhesive
- ☐ 10 inches (25.4 cm) of peach satin ribbon, ¼ inch (6 mm) wide
- ☐ 1-inch (2.5 cm) clear button
- ☐ tape

Busy lives make time precious, so reward someone who has offered his or her time with a kind gesture of your own.

INSTRUCTIONS

1. Create holes around the edge of the brown circle card with the $\frac{1}{16}$-inch (1.5 mm) hole punch, $\frac{1}{4}$-inch (3 mm) hole punch, and $\frac{1}{4}$-inch (6 mm) hole punch, about $\frac{1}{4}$ inch (6 mm) from the edges.

2. Adhere the flower to the center of the circle card with mini glue dots. Attach the clock transparency to the center of the flower with one mini glue dot.

3. Using a computer with word processing software, print "thank you for your time" onto white cardstock. Cut text block to 1 inch tall x $2\frac{1}{2}$ inches wide (2.5 x 6.4 cm). Trim peach paper to $1\frac{1}{4}$ inch tall x $2\frac{3}{4}$ inches wide (3.2 x 7 cm). Center and adhere the message onto the peach paper.

4. Tie a knot in the center of the peach ribbon. Thread each end of the ribbon through one of the holes in the button, pulling until the knot rests in the middle of the button. Punch a $\frac{1}{8}$-inch (3 mm) hole in the upper left corner of the message tag. String the tag onto the ribbon end on the right side of the card.

5. Adhere the button and ribbon to the center of the clock using a mini glue dot. Tape the ends of the ribbon to the underside of the card. Cut a circle slightly smaller than the chocolate circle card out of the peach paper and adhere it to the back side of the card to hide the ribbon ends. Secure the message tag in place on the front of the card with a mini glue dot.

Giving a Hoot

by RENÉE DeBLOIS

SUPPLIES

Tools

- [ ] paper trimmer or cutting mat, craft knife, and ruler
- [ ] bone folder
- [ ] foam brush
- [ ] owl stamp
- [ ] computer with word processing software and printer
- [ ] ⅛-inch (3 mm) hole punch

Materials

- [ ] watercolor cardstock or card
- [ ] adhesive
- [ ] fine pink glitter
- [ ] two pale pink brads

Thanks for giving a hoot and a holler!

Recognize a loved one or a friend who simply took the time to listen and to care.

INSTRUCTIONS

1. Cut the watercolor cardstock to 5¾ inches tall x 10 inches wide (14.6 x 25.4 cm). Score and fold the card with the bone folder to create a 5¾-inch-tall x 5-inch-wide (14.6 x 12.7 cm) card base (card opens from the right). Paper-tear the right edge of the card. Use the foam brush to lightly coat the owl stamp with a adhesive. Center and stamp the owl image onto front of card. Immediately cover the image with pink glitter. Allow it to dry overnight.

2. Using a computer with word processing software, type "Thanks for giving a hoot and a holler." Adjust the font color to pink. Print the message onto watercolor cardstock and cut it out to a ¾-inch-tall x 4⅞-inch-wide (1.9 x 12.4 cm) strip. Center and adhere the message to the front of the card, layering it over the owl.

3. Use ⅛-inch (3 mm) hole punch to punch two holes to the right and left sides of the phrase. Attach it with the pale pink brads.

Your Kindness

by KIM KESTI

Be as thoughtful as they were kind with this cheerful thank you note.

How beautiful a day can be
when kindness touches it!
~George Elliston

SUPPLIES

Tools

- [ ] paper trimmer or a cutting mat, craft knife, and ruler
- [ ] bone folder
- [ ] computer with word processing software and printer
- [ ] popsicle stick

Materials

- [ ] dark brown cardstock
- [ ] striped patterned paper
- [ ] leaf-motif patterned paper
- [ ] adhesive
- [ ] white cardstock
- [ ] brown border design rub-on
- [ ] square felt leaf-motif embellishment

INSTRUCTIONS

1. Cut the dark brown cardstock to 7 inches tall x 7 inches wide (17.8 x 17.8 cm). Score with the bone folder, creating a 3½-inch-tall x 7-inch-wide (8.9 x 17.8 cm) card base. Trim the striped patterned paper to 3 inches tall x 7 inches wide (7.6 x 17.8 cm). Cut the leaf-motif patterned paper to 2 inches tall x 7 inches wide (5 x 17.8 cm).

TIP: Card opens from the bottom.

3. Print the quote onto white cardstock. Trim the message to 1½ inches tall x 5 inches wide (3.8 x 12.7 cm). Using a ruler to guide placement, use a popsicle stick to transfer the brown border rub-on at the top and bottom of the white cardstock. Center and adhere this piece to the left side of the front of the card.

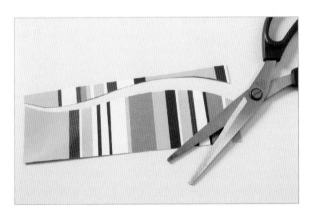

2. Cut a wavy edge at the top and bottom of the striped patterned paper. Center and adhere it to the front of the card. Adhere the leaf-motif patterned paper on top of the striped paper on the card.

4. Adhere the felt leaf-motif embellishment to the right of the white cardstock.

A Perfect Day

by CANDICE CRUZ

Show someone how much your time together meant to you with this picture journey card.

SUPPLIES

Tools

- ☐ ⅛-inch (3 mm) hole punch
- ☐ bone folder
- ☐ computer with word processing software and printer

Materials

- ☐ 10 index photo prints
- ☐ plastic gum container, 2 inches tall x 3 inches wide (5 x 7.6 cm)
- ☐ striped patterned paper
- ☐ 18 inches (45.6 cm) peach-colored satin ribbon, ¼-inch (6 mm) wide
- ☐ white cardstock
- ☐ green crocheted blossom embellishment
- ☐ white chipboard
- ☐ cardstock tags
- ☐ paper word tags such as "memories" and "adore"
- ☐ foam adhesive
- ☐ mini glue dots
- ☐ tape

INSTRUCTIONS

1. Cut the white cardstock into a 1½-inch-tall x 12-inch-wide (3.8 x 30.4 cm) strip. Trim the patterned paper into pieces: Cut four 1½-inch-tall x 2-inch-wide (3.8 x 5 cm) pieces. Cut two 1½-inch-tall x 2½-inch-wide (3.8 x 6.4 cm) pieces. Cut one 1¾-inch-tall x 2¾-inch-wide (4.4 x 7 cm) piece. Cut one 1½-inch-tall x 2¾-inch-wide (3.8 x 7 cm) piece. Cut the chipboard into one 1½-inch-tall x 2½-inch-wide (3.8 x 6.4 cm) piece.

TIP: Cut all pieces so the stripes are horizontal.

2. Crease the white cardstock strip into an accordion with the bone folder, creating six 2-inch (5 cm) sections. The leftmost section will nest into the gum container with the accordion trailing out.

3. Lay the white cardstock accordion flat. Adhere three of the four 1½-inch-tall x 2-inch-wide (3.8 x 5 cm) patterned paper pieces to the first, third, and fifth sections of the accordion. Punch a ⅛-inch (3 mm) hole in the center of the fourth 1½-inch-tall x 2-inch-wide (3.8 x 5 cm) patterned paper piece. Cut a piece of peach satin ribbon into a 3-inch (7.6 cm) length and fold it in half. Thread the folded part of the ribbon up through the hole so that about ½ inch (1.3 cm) sticks out and creates a loop on the patterned paper side. Tape the ribbon ends down on the back of the patterned paper. Adhere this paper and ribbon piece to the sixth section of the accordion but on the side opposite the other patterned pieces.

TIP: The patterned paper with ribbon loop allows you to pull the accordion out of the container.

4. Cut the index photo prints out, leaving a ⅛-inch (3 mm) white border around the images. Adhere the photos to the sections of the accordion as desired. You might add a paper tag with words that fit your theme such as "adore."

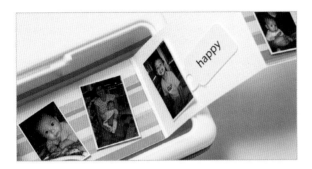

5. Empty the plastic gum container and peel off the labels. Line the bottom of the container with the 1½-inch-tall x 2¾-inch-wide (3.8 x 7 cm) piece of patterned paper, adhering it with glue dots. Then attach the leftmost section of the accordion to the inside bottom of the plastic container using glue dots. Fold the accordion up into the container.

6. Using a computer with word processing software, print the words "Thanks for a perfect day!" onto white cardstock. Cut the words into individual blocks about ½ inch (1.3 cm) tall. Adhere the words to a 1½-inch-tall x 2½-inch-wide (3.8 x 6.4 cm) piece of patterned paper. Attach this to the inside flap of the container's cover. Close the lid.

7. Adhere the 1½-inch-tall x 2½-inch-wide (3.8 x 6.4 cm) piece of chipboard to the top of the gum container. Cover the chipboard with a piece of patterned paper, 1½ inches tall x 2½ inches wide (3.8 x 6.4 cm).

8. Cut a piece of peach ribbon to 4 inches (10.2 cm) long and trim the ends at an angle. Tie a knot in the center of the ribbon. Feed the ends of the ribbon into the crocheted flower so the knot rests in the center of the flower and the ribbon ends fan out underneath the flower. Adhere the crocheted flower with ribbon to the front of the container using glue dots. Adhere the "memories" paper tag to the right of the flower.

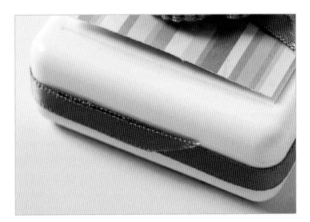

9. Cut an 11-inch (27.9 cm) piece of peach ribbon. Adhere it along the outer rim of the container using mini glue dots.

Being There

by KIM KESTI

This is the thank you note for the consistent "go-to" person in your life.

THANKS FOR
ALWAYS BEING
THERE

SUPPLIES

Tools

☐ paper trimmer or cutting mat, craft knife, and ruler

☐ bone folder

☐ pencil

☐ small square punch

☐ computer with word processing software and printer

☐ 1½-inch (3.8 cm) circle punch

Materials

☐ yellow cardstock

☐ yellow and teal floral patterned paper

☐ 14 inches (35.6 cm) of dotted yellow ribbon, ⅜ inch (9.5 mm) wide

☐ window mount frame

☐ adhesive

☐ foam tape

☐ yellow rivets

☐ teal flowers

INSTRUCTIONS

1. Trim the yellow cardstock to 4½ inches tall x 11¾ inches wide (11.4 x 29.8 cm). Measure points at 5½ inches (14 cm) and 11 inches (27.9 cm) from the left. Score the cardstock at these points with the bone folder. Fold the cardstock in from the left to the 5½-inch (14 cm) point. Fold the cardstock in from the right to the 11-inch (27.9 cm) point. Folds should create a "matchbook."

2. Punch a small square hole in the center of the matchbook fold. Thread the dotted yellow ribbon through the hole and tie it in a bow.

3. Frame a 4-inch (10.2 cm) square piece of floral yellow paper behind the window mount frame. Adhere it to the front of the card.

4. Use a computer with word processing software and print "Thanks for always being there" onto yellow cardstock. Punch out the sentiment with a 1½-inch (3.8 cm) circle punch. Adhere it to the bottom right window with foam tape.

5. Snap rivets onto the three teal flowers. Use foam tape to attach them to the other three windows.

Lending a Hand

by **KELLY PURKEY**

This colorful 3-D stand-up card practically applauds your friend or loved one for helping out.

SUPPLIES

Tools

- [ ] paper trimmer or cutting mat, craft knife, and ruler
- [ ] pencil
- [ ] scissors
- [ ] bone folder

Materials

- [ ] white cardstock
- [ ] green cardstock
- [ ] 13 inches (33 cm) of striped ribbon, ⅜ inch (9.5 mm) wide
- [ ] ribbon tape

- [ ] tape runner
- [ ] three types of patterned paper
- [ ] black lowercase alphabet stickers
- [ ] six ¼-inch (6 mm) round brads

INSTRUCTIONS

1. Cut a 2½-inch-tall x 12-inch-wide (6.4 x 30.4 cm) strip of white cardstock. Trim a 1-inch-tall x 12-inch-wide (2.5 x 30.4 cm) strip of green cardstock. Trace your hand (upside down or right side up depending on which direction you want the thumb to point) onto the back of each of the three patterned papers and cut out the three hand shapes.

2. Adhere the green cardstock strip to the bottom of the white cardstock. Adhere the striped ribbon above the green strip, leaving ½ inch (1.3 cm) of ribbon hanging off each edge. Fold the ribbon over and adhere it to the back of card.

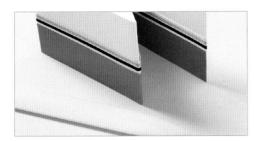

3. Mark 4-inch (10.2 cm) sections for folds with a ruler and pencil. Crease and score the card into an accordion fold with the bone folder.

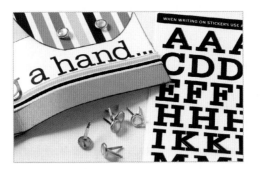

4. Apply the black alphabet stickers above the ribbon to write "thank you for lending a hand . . ." on the card. The "thank you" fits in the first section; "for lending" has the "g" a little past the crease on the second section; and "a hand . . ." fits in the third section. Apply adhesive to the bottom of the back of the hand cut-outs. Glue a hand in the center of each section of the card. Push two brads through the bottoms of each hand and secure them on the back of the card.

Sticking Your Neck Out

by WENDY WHITE

It takes guts to stick up for people you care about,

so show your appreciation with this fun giraffe card.

SUPPLIES

Tools

☐ paper trimmer or cutting mat, craft knife, and ruler

☐ bone folder

☐ popsicle stick

☐ scissors

☐ computer with word processing software and printer

☐ small paint brush

Materials

☐ blue cardstock

☐ light green cardstock

☐ dark green cardstock

☐ clear "paper" (thick vellum or thin plastic sheet)

☐ "Thank You" rub-on

☐ adhesive

☐ giraffe sticker

☐ printable transparency

☐ white paint

INSTRUCTIONS

1. Cut the blue cardstock to 3 inches tall x 8½ inches wide (7.6 x 21.6 cm). Trim a piece of light green cardstock to 1½ inches tall x 2¾ inches wide (3.8 x 7 cm). Cut a piece of dark green cardstock to 1¼ inches tall x 2½ inches (3.2 x 6.4 cm) wide. Cut a piece of thick clear "paper" to 5½ inches tall x 4⅛ inches wide (14 x 10.5 cm).

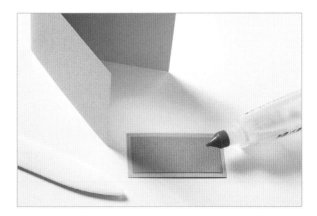

2. Score the blue cardstock with the bone folder, creating a card base measuring 3 inches tall x 4¼ inches wide (7.6 x 10.8 cm). Center and adhere the dark green cardstock rectangle on top of the light green cardstock rectangle.

TIP: Card opens from the right.

3. Use the popsicle stick to transfer the "Thank You" rub-on to the center of the green rectangle piece. Apply adhesive to the bottom half of this rectangle. Glue it to the front of the card. The top half of the rectangle should stick out over the top of the blue card base.

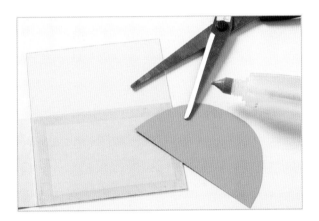

4. Glue the bottom half of the thick clear "paper" to the inside of the blue card base. Cut a piece of dark green cardstock to 2½ inches tall x 4¼ inches wide (6.4 x 10.8 cm). Round the top with scissors to create a "hill." Center and glue the "hill" on top of the clear "paper" at the bottom of the inside of the card.

5. Place the giraffe sticker on top of the "hill." Check placement before sticking to ensure the head of the giraffe will be visible when you close the card. Using a computer with word processing software, write "for sticking your neck out for me." Adjust the colors so that the words are blue with a black outline. Print the message onto the inkjet transparency. Cut out the words and glue them over the legs of the giraffe.

6. Paint white dots around the perimeter of the clear "paper." Allow the paint to dry.

The Cash

by WENDY WHITE

Tell them how you spent the green they gave you with this whimsical card.

SUPPLIES

Tools

☐ paper trimmer or cutting mat, craft knife, and ruler

☐ computer with word processing software and printer

☐ bone folder

☐ something round to trace

☐ pencil

☐ scissors

Materials

☐ green cardstock

☐ burgundy patterned paper

☐ white cardstock

☐ adhesive

☐ "$" chipboard accent

INSTRUCTIONS

1. Cut the green cardstock to 8½ inches tall x 5½ inches wide (21.6 x 14 cm). Trim one piece of burgundy patterned paper to 2 inches tall x 4 inches wide (5 x 10.2 cm). Cut another piece of burgundy paper to 4¼ inches tall x 5½ inches wide (10.8 x 14 cm). Cut the white cardstock to 3 inches tall x 5½ inches wide (7.6 x 14 cm).

2. Fold and score the 8½-inch-tall x 5½-inch-wide (21.6 x 14 cm) green cardstock to create a card base that is 4¼ inches tall x 5½ inches wide (10.8 x 14 cm) (opens from the bottom). Adhere the white cardstock to the front of the card, about ½ inch (1.3 cm) up from the bottom edge.

3. Place something round along the left edge of the burgundy 2-inch-tall x 4-inch-wide (5 x 10.2 cm) cardstock. Trace a half-circle and trim the curved edge with scissors, making sure the pattern is visible.

4. Adhere the burgundy piece to the front of the card, aligned to the right. Center and adhere the "$" chipboard accent to the burgundy piece on the front of the card.

5. Adhere the 4¼-inch-tall x 5½-inch-wide (10.8 x 14 cm) burgundy patterned paper to the inside panel. Using a computer with word processing software, write "Thanks for the cash. . . . It was my favorite color!" Print these words onto green cardstock and trim the paper to 2 inches tall x 4 inches wide (5 x 10.2 cm). Trace a half-circle on the left edge and cut it out. Adhere the message to the inside of the card, aligned to the right.

The Flowers

by RENÉE DeBLOIS

Let this adorable penguin do the thanking for you.

INSTRUCTIONS

1. Use black ink to stamp the penguin with flower image onto the white cardstock. Color the beak and feet with an orange marker. Color the lower edge of the belly with the light blue marker. Punch out image using 2½-inch (6.4 cm) circle punch.

TIP: Look at the underside of the punch when punching to ensure the image is centered.

2. Ink the edges of the cut-out circle with the purple ink. Put a little glue on the edges and sprinkle on glitter.

3. Use the 3-inch (7.6 cm) scallop punch to punch a circle out of the white cardstock. Using ⅛-inch (3 mm) hole punch, punch holes in each scallop.

4. Glue the penguin circle onto the scalloped circle. Create a slit in the fold of the pink note card with the craft knife, about one-third of the way down from the top. Feed the red silk ribbon through a hole on the right side of the scalloped circle edge and back up through another hole on the opposite side. Thread the ribbon through the slit and loop it around the inside of the card. Tie a knot in the ribbon in the front of the card. Use glue dots to adhere the scallop piece to the front of the card.

5. Using the popsicle stick, rub on letters to spell "thanks for the flowers" at the bottom of the card.

6. Attach the white brad to the center of the purple flower embellishment. Adhere the flower to the front of the card.

Your Sympathy

by RENÉE DeBLOIS

SUPPLIES

Tools

☐ paper trimmer or cutting mat, craft knife, and ruler

☐ scissors

☐ computer with word processing software and printer

☐ pencil

☐ popsicle stick

☐ bone folder

Materials

☐ pink "petal" card

☐ two different kinds of patterned paper

☐ adhesive

☐ bird design patterned paper

☐ glue pen

☐ ultra-fine glitter

☐ wax paper

☐ foam mounting tape

☐ hot pink alphabet rub-ons

☐ vellum

☐ white cardstock

☐ 18 inches (45.6 cm) of hot pink ribbon, ¼ inch (6 mm) wide

A friend or a loved one who is sympathetic during a difficult time can be thanked with this intricate card.

INSTRUCTIONS

1. Trace the semicircle flaps of the petal card onto two different patterned papers (creating two of each). Cut them out and adhere them to the outside of the card on the petals.

2. Using a computer with word processing software, type "Thanks for your sympathy." Adjust the color to dark blue, and print the message onto patterned paper. Cut to a 5⅛-inch (13 cm) square. Trace the glue pen around an element of the patterned paper inside the card and cover it with glitter. Allow it to dry, then adhere it to the inside of the petal card.

3. Cut the bird design out of the patterned paper. Lightly cover the bird face with glue. Place it face-up on the wax paper and sprinkle it with fine glitter. Tap off the excess glitter. Allow it to dry. Adhere the foam mounting tape to the underside of the bird, and stick it on the front of the card.

TIP: Make sure the petal card can close before attaching the bird to the front of the card.

4. Use the popsicle stick to transfer the hot pink "thank you" rub-ons to the white cardstock. Cut cardstock into a 5⁄8-inch (1.6 cm) square. Use foam tape to adhere the message to the card underneath the bird's beak.

5. Cut a strip of vellum 2 inches tall x 11 inches wide (5 x 27.9 cm). Wrap the vellum around the card. Adhere the ends on the back of the card and trim off any excess vellum. Tie the hot pink ribbon around the card, ending with a bow at the front.

The Gift

by WENDY WHITE

SUPPLIES

Tools

- ☐ paper trimmer or cutting mat, craft knife, and ruler
- ☐ bone folder
- ☐ "girl with present" stamp
- ☐ scissors
- ☐ computer with word processing software and printer

Materials

- ☐ light black cardstock
- ☐ plaid patterned paper
- ☐ black ink
- ☐ pink cardstock
- ☐ clear transparency
- ☐ black pen
- ☐ adhesive

This pink and plaid thank you note is sure to delight as much as the gift did.

INSTRUCTIONS

1. Cut a piece of light black cardstock to 5½ inches tall x 8½ inches wide (14 x 21.6 cm). Trim a second piece of light black cardstock to 3¾ inches tall x 3⅝ inches wide (9.5 x 9.2 cm). Cut the plaid patterned paper into two pieces, each measuring 5¼ inches tall x 4 inches wide (13.3 x 10.2 cm).

3. Use black ink to stamp the "girl with present" image onto the pink cardstock. Trim the pink cardstock with this stamped image to 3½ inches tall x 2½ inches wide (8.9 x 6.4 cm), leaving a border around the image.

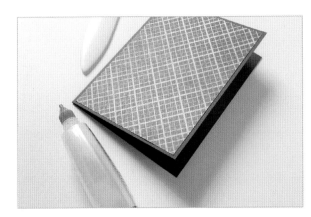

2. Score and fold the larger light black cardstock with the bone folder to create a card base that is 5½ inches tall x 4¼ inches wide (14 x 10.8 cm) (card opens from the right). Center and adhere one piece of plaid patterned paper to the front of the card base.

4. Take a scrap piece of the plaid patterned paper and turn it face down, showing the white backside. Use black ink to stamp "girl with present" image onto the piece of clear transparency. Use this to "stamp" on the scrap paper, creating a mirror image of the stamp.

TIP: Do not use ink that dries quickly.

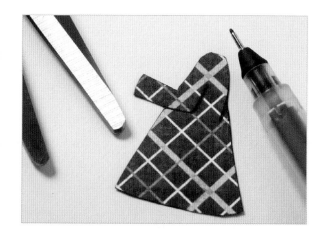

5. Cut the dress out of the plaid patterned paper. Use the black pen to line the edges and add the detail of the coat's arm line. Adhere this piece to the stamped image of the coat on the pink cardstock. Glue down only the top part of the coat. Curl the bottom of the coat for a 3-D effect. Mat the pink cardstock with the stamped girl image to the smaller piece of light black cardstock. Center and adhere it to the front of the card.

6. Using a computer with word processing software, type "Thank You for the gift." Print the message on pink cardstock and trim it to $4\frac{1}{2}$ inches tall x $3\frac{1}{4}$ inches wide (11.4 x 8.3 cm), with the sentiment at the top. Mount it onto the plaid patterned paper. Center and adhere this to the inside of card.

Spreading Sunshine

by KELLY PURKEY

If you know someone who shines as brightly as the sun, this is the warmest card to give.

SUPPLIES

Tools

- ☐ paper trimmer or cutting mat, craft knife, and ruler
- ☐ bone folder
- ☐ wave pattern decorative-edged scissors
- ☐ flower punch
- ☐ scissors

Materials

- ☐ white cardstock
- ☐ cloud patterned paper
- ☐ adhesive
- ☐ brownish green "linen" patterned paper
- ☐ pop-up glue dots
- ☐ plastic sun embellishment

- ☐ orange and yellow brads
- ☐ green cardstock
- ☐ pink cardstock
- ☐ 5 inches (12.7 cm) of green polka dot ribbon, ⅜ inch (9.5 mm) wide
- ☐ small square colorful alphabet stickers

INSTRUCTIONS

1. Cut the white cardstock to 4 inches tall x 12 inches wide (10.2 x 30.4 cm). Score and fold the cardstock with the bone folder to create a 4-inch-tall x 6-inch-wide (10.2 x 15.2 cm) card base (card opens from the right). Cut a 4-inch-tall x 6-inch-wide (10.2 x 15.2 cm) piece of cloud patterned paper. Adhere it to the inside of the card

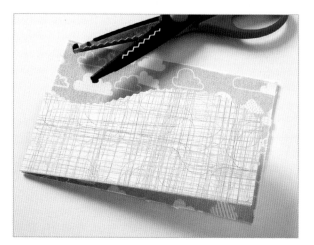

2. Cut a 4-inch-tall x 6-inch-wide (10.2 x 15.2 cm) piece of brownish green "linen" patterned paper. Adhere this paper to the front of the card. Use wave pattern decorative-edged scissors to cut a wave out of the front of the card. The cloud patterned paper on the inside will be visible. Use regular scissors to cut and remove the top of the front of the card.

3. Use pop-up glue dots to adhere the plastic sun to the top left of the cloud patterned paper. Attach the yellow brad inside the center of the sun.

4. Cut five 2-inch-tall x ⅛-inch-wide (5 cm x 3 mm) strips of the green cardstock to create flower stems. Adhere them to the front of the card about 1 inch (2.5 cm) apart. Use the flower punch to create five flowers out of pink cardstock. Adhere one flower to the top of each stem. Attach an orange brad through the center of each flower. Cut the green polka dot ribbon into ten ½-inch (1.3 cm) lengths. Cut the ends on an angle. Adhere the ribbon to each side of the flower stems.

5. Use stickers to spell "Thanks For Spreading Sunshine" on the front of the card.

CHAPTER 4

Thankful for Your Love Cards

Love is something to be grateful for each and every day, for life *is* love. There are a million ways we show our love every day: in the gentle words that we use, the small kindnesses that we offer a friend or loved one, and in the thoughtfulness and care we give to each other. Whether you choose to create a handmade card that is romantic, heartfelt, silly, or cute, a thank you note is really just another way of saying "I love you."

Thanks for Your Love

by RENÉE DeBLOIS

SUPPLIES

Tools

- [ ] computer with word processing software and printer
- [ ] pencil
- [ ] scissors
- [ ] paper trimmer or cutting mat, craft knife, and ruler

Materials

- [ ] photo paper
- [ ] adhesive
- [ ] four small and one larger tin tile embellishments
- [ ] 1¼-inch (3.2 cm) square photo
- [ ] foam mounting tape
- [ ] flocked blue note card

A modern, personal expression perfect for any loved one.

INSTRUCTIONS

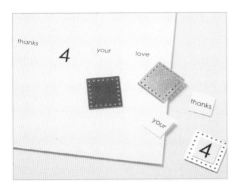

1. Using a computer with word processing software, type "thanks," "4," "your," and "love." Adjust font color to navy blue. Print the words onto photo paper and allow them to dry. Trim them to ½-inch (1.3 cm) squares and adhere the words to the small tin tiles.

2. Adhere the photo to the larger tin tile embellishment. Use foam mounting tape to adhere the photo on tin in the window of the flocked blue note card.

3. Use the ruler to align placement of the four small tins at the bottom of the card. Adhere them using foam mounting tape. Place the "thanks" and "love" tiles first to ensure correct placement.

You Rock

by WENDY WHITE

This spinning card will rock their world, just like they do yours.

SUPPLIES

Tools

- ☐ 1½-inch (3.8 cm) circle punch
- ☐ ¾-inch (1.9 cm) circle punch
- ☐ ⅝-inch (1.6 cm) circle punch
- ☐ bone folder
- ☐ popsicle stick

Materials

- ☐ black cardstock
- ☐ orange cardstock
- ☐ yellow cardstock
- ☐ pop-up glue dots

- ☐ blue foam alphabet stickers ("y," "o," "u," "r," "o," "c," "k")
- ☐ eight pennies
- ☐ rub-on letters to spell "couldn't do it without you"

INSTRUCTIONS

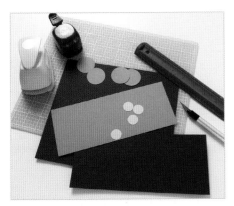

1. Cut a piece of black cardstock to 8 inches tall x 9 inches wide (20.3 x 22.9 cm). Trim a second piece of black cardstock to $3\frac{7}{8}$ inches tall x $8\frac{7}{8}$ inches wide (9.8 x 22.5 cm). Cut a piece of orange cardstock to $3\frac{1}{2}$ inches tall x $8\frac{1}{2}$ inches wide (8.9 x 21.6 cm). Punch four $1\frac{1}{2}$-inch (3. 8 cm) circles from orange cardstock. Punch out four $\frac{3}{4}$-inch (1.9 cm) circles from yellow cardstock.

2. Center and glue a yellow circle onto each orange circle. Place a blue foam alphabet sticker—"r," "o," "c," "k"—onto each circle.

3. Use the $\frac{5}{8}$-inch (1.6 cm) circle punch to create four equally spaced holes across the $3\frac{7}{8}$-inch-tall x $8\frac{7}{8}$-inch-wide (9.8 x 22.5 cm) black cardstock.

4. Put a pop-up glue dot on each of four pennies. Lay the black cardstock with the holes in it over the pennies so the pop-up glue dots poke through each of the holes. Stick a second penny on top of each of the first pennies. The black cardstock will be sandwiched between the pennies. Glue one of each of the circles with the foam letters on top of each penny, spelling "rock."

5. Score the 8-inch-tall x 9-inch-wide (20.3 x 22.9 cm) piece of black cardstock and fold it to create a 4-inch-tall x 9-inch-wide (10.2 x 22.9 cm) card base. Put pop-up glue dots along the perimeter of the back of the black cardstock with the "rock" lettering. Layer the black cardstock piece onto the front of the card. Adhere foam letters spelling "you" above the "rock".

TIP: Card opens from the bottom.

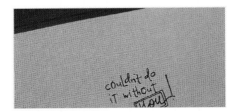

6. Center and adhere the orange cardstock piece to the inside of the card. There will be a small black border around the edge. Use the popsicle stick to transfer rub-ons that read "couldn't do it without you" onto the center of the orange cardstock.

With All My Heart

by WENDY WHITE

Thank them from the bottom of your heart and soul.

I thank you

SUPPLIES

Tools

- [ ] paper trimmer or cutting mat, craft knife, and ruler
- [ ] pencil
- [ ] bone folder
- [ ] popsicle stick

Materials

- [ ] light yellow cardstock
- [ ] scalloped-edged blue polka dot patterned paper
- [ ] adhesive

- [ ] rub-ons or stickers to spell "I thank you" and "With all my heart"
- [ ] pink heart die-cut accent
- [ ] pop-up glue dots

INSTRUCTIONS

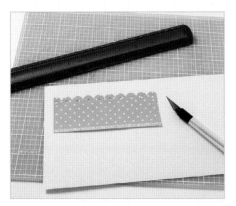

1. Cut the light yellow cardstock to 10 inches tall x 5½ inches wide (25.4 x 14 cm). Trim the scalloped-edged blue polka dot paper to 2 inches tall x 5½ inches wide (5 x 14 cm).

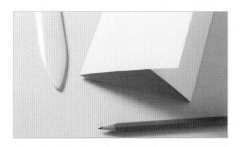

2. With a pencil and bone folder, mark and score the light yellow cardstock at 2 inches (5 cm) and 6 inches (15.2 cm). Fold the cardstock along the score lines with the bone folder to create a card base with flap. Erase the pencil marks.

3. Adhere the blue polka dot paper to the 2-inch (5 cm) flap of the light yellow card base, with the scalloped edge as the bottom.

4. Use the popsicle stick to transfer the "I thank you" rub-on to the center of the pink heart die-cut accent.

5. Put pop-up glue dots on the bottom half of the back of the heart. Adhere the heart to the light yellow cardstock.

TIP: Check your placement before attaching. The top part of the heart should overlap the flap and hold it shut.

6. Inside the card, transfer rub-ons to spell "With all my heart."

From the Bottom of My Heart

by KELLY PURKEY

This big red and pink heart says "thank you" with all the trimmings.

SUPPLIES

Tools

- ☐ paper trimmer or cutting mat, craft knife, and ruler
- ☐ scissors
- ☐ sewing machine
- ☐ scalloped-edge decorative scissors
- ☐ flower stamp
- ☐ bone folder
- ☐ pencil

Materials

- ☐ red cardstock
- ☐ white cardstock
- ☐ adhesive
- ☐ brown thread
- ☐ pink cardstock
- ☐ black ink pad
- ☐ brown brads

- ☐ five kinds of coordinating patterned paper
- ☐ white alphabet stickers
- ☐ brown pen
- ☐ 15 inches (38.1 cm) of red ribbon, 7⁄8 inch (2.2 cm) wide
- ☐ glue dots
- ☐ stick pin with heart accent

INSTRUCTIONS

1. Cut a 4½-inch-tall x 6¼-inch-wide (11.4 x 15.9 cm) heart out of the red cardstock. Mount the heart onto the white cardstock and cut around the heart, creating a ¼-inch (6 mm) white border. Use the sewing machine with brown thread to sew a zigzag stitch where the red and white cardstock meet. Mount the heart onto the pink cardstock. Cut out the heart with scalloped decorative scissors, leaving a ½-inch (1.3 cm) pink border around the heart.

2. Use the flower stamp and black ink to stamp a border of flowers around the red part of the heart. Stamp images about 1 inch (2.5 cm) apart. Attach the brown brads between the flowers.

3. Cut a 2½-inch-tall x 12-inch-wide (6.4 x 30.4 cm) strip of white cardstock. Mark 2-inch (5 cm) sections for folds with a ruler and pencil. Use the bone folder to crease and score the card into an accordion fold with six sections. Cut 2-inch-tall x 2½-inch-wide (5 x 6.4 cm) pieces of five different kinds of coordinating patterned paper. Adhere one piece to each section of the accordion. There will be one "empty" section at the bottom.

4. Adhere the white alphabet stickers to the five patterned accordion sections, spelling "thanks" "from" "the" "bottom" "of my" from the top down. Outline the white letter stickers with the brown pen.

5. Cut a ¾-inch-tall x 2½-inch-wide (1.3 x 6.4 cm) strip of white cardstock and trim the top edge with the scalloped-edge scissors. Adhere this piece to the top section of the accordion strip. Sew them together with brown thread.

6. Adhere the "empty" section of the accordion strip to the center of the red heart, making sure the accordion will fold correctly before gluing it down. Use glue dots to adhere red ribbon to the back of the heart. Fold up the accordion and tie the ribbon in a knot in the front of the heart. Stick a pin with a heart accent through the center of the knot.

Two Birdies with Banner

by RENÉE DeBLOIS

These sweet little birdies bring thanks to a loved one or friend.

SUPPLIES

Tools

- ☐ paper trimmer or cutting mat, craft knife, and ruler
- ☐ bone folder
- ☐ scissors
- ☐ birds with "thanks" stamp

Materials

- ☐ pale aqua cardstock
- ☐ pink and white patterned paper
- ☐ adhesive
- ☐ pink eyelet stationery
- ☐ 10 inches (25.4 cm) of black decorative ribbon, ⅛ inch (3 mm) wide
- ☐ tape
- ☐ black ink
- ☐ white cardstock
- ☐ foam mounting tape

INSTRUCTIONS

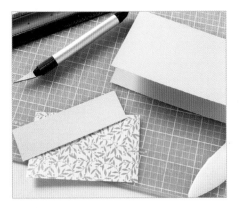

1. Cut the pale aqua cardstock to 7 inches tall x 4⅞ inches wide (17.8 x 12.4 cm). Using the bone folder, score and fold the cardstock to create a card base measuring 3½ inches tall x 4⅞ inches wide (8.9 x 12.4 cm). (Card opens from the bottom). Trim a second piece of pale aqua cardstock to 1¼ inches tall x 4⅛ inches wide (3.2 x 10.5 cm). Cut the pink and white patterned paper to 2½ inches tall x 4 inches wide (6.4 x 10.2 cm).

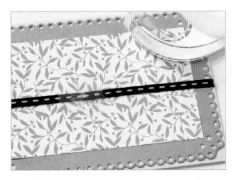

2. Adhere the pink eyelet stationery card to the front of the pale aqua card base. Wrap the ribbon around the card, taping the ribbon ends down at the front of the card.

3. Stamp the birds with "thanks" image on the white cardstock. Cut it to 1 inch tall x 3⅞ inches wide (2.5 x 9.8 cm). Center the bird image and adhere it to the smaller piece of pale aqua cardstock using the foam mounting tape.

So Sweet

by KELLY PURKEY

SUPPLIES

Tools

☐ paper trimmer or cutting mat, craft knife, and ruler

☐ scalloped-edged decorative scissors

☐ popsicle stick

☐ scissors

☐ ¼-inch (6 mm) hole punch

Materials

☐ patterned paper

☐ pink paper

☐ adhesive

☐ rub-ons to read "Thanks for being so sweet "

☐ rub-on bird design

☐ white cardstock

☐ 5 inches (12.7 cm) of blue and white striped ribbon, ⅜ inch (9.5 mm) wide

☐ 5-inch tall x 3¼-inch wide (12.7 cm x 8.3) plastic bag

☐ assorted candy

☐ green brads

Candies are the perfect little thank you gift for someone who is sweet to you.

INSTRUCTIONS

1. Cut a 5-inch-tall x 3⅞-inch-wide (12.7 x 9.8 cm) piece of patterned paper. Fold it in half. Cut a ½-inch-tall x 3⅞-inch-wide (1.3 x 9.8 cm) strip of pink paper. Use scalloped-edged decorative scissors to cut the bottom edge of the pink paper. Adhere the pink paper to the bottom front of the folded patterned paper.

2. Transfer "Thanks for being so sweet" rub-ons to the white cardstock with a popsicle stick. Cut the following words into three separate strips: "Thanks," "for being," and "so sweet." Adhere the strips to the left side of the patterned paper.

3. Punch two holes through the folded top of the patterned paper, 1 inch (2.5 cm) from each end. Loop the blue and white striped ribbon through the holes and tie it in a knot.

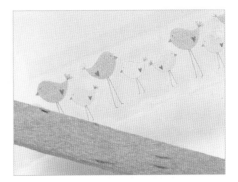

4. Transfer the bird rub-ons with a popsicle stick along the bottom of the plastic bag. Fill the bag with assorted candy.

5. Cover the top of the plastic bag with the patterned paper piece. Attach the green brads ½ inch (1.3 cm) from the edges of the paper.

Thank You for Loving Me

by CANDICE CRUZ

Being thankful for someone's love is cause for celebration with this card.

SUPPLIES

Tools

- ☐ paper trimmer or cutting mat, craft knife, and ruler
- ☐ die-cut machine and heart die-cut
- ☐ sewing machine
- ☐ bone folder
- ☐ computer with word processing software and printer
- ☐ corner rounder

Materials

- ☐ black cardstock
- ☐ red cardstock
- ☐ self-adhesive "couple" patterned fabric
- ☐ black thread
- ☐ mini glue dots
- ☐ black liquid appliqué

- ☐ self-adhesive rhinestones
- ☐ white cardstock
- ☐ tape
- ☐ clear plastic arrow
- ☐ foam mounting tape

INSTRUCTIONS

1. Cut the black cardstock to 8½ inches tall x 5½ inches wide (21.6 x 14 cm). Cut the red cardstock to 2½ inches (6.4 cm) square. Use a die-cut machine to cut a heart out of the self-adhesive patterned fabric.

2. Starting at the bottom of the heart, sew a zigzag stitch around the edges of the heart with black thread. Score and fold the black cardstock with a bone folder to form a 4¼-inch-tall x 5½-inch-wide card base (10.8 x 14 cm). (Card opens from the bottom). Adhere the heart to the card with mini glue dots, allowing part of the heart to hang off the edge of the card.

3. Use the black liquid appliqué to draw circles around the "couple" on the patterned fabric closest to the center of the heart. Allow the circles to dry. Adhere the rhinestone circles onto the black circle drawn with the liquid appliqué.

4. Using a computer, create a 2-inch (5 cm) square. Fill the shape with a black background. Create a text box, and type the phrase "thank you for [leave a couple of empty lines] me the way you do." Create another text box and type the word "loving" using a script font in a larger size. Center it between the other text lines. Change all font colors to white and print the message onto white cardstock.

5. Cut the printed message out of the white cardstock. Use the corner rounder to round the edges of this piece and the cut-out red cardstock square. Adhere the message square to the red cardstock.

6. Tape the end of the clear plastic arrow to the back of the message square. Use the foam mounting squares to attach the message square and arrow to the bottom right corner of the card.

CHAPTER 5

Thanks, Just Because Cards

How wonderful when a thank you note is a gift in itself. A simple way to show our gratefulness for the world around us, the act of creating a handmade card "just because" reminds us (and others) that we are able to give and receive love. The knowledge fills us with gratitude for the people, places, and experiences we have in our lives. When we use thank you notes in everyday life as a way to honor and celebrate our lives and each other, they can be a divine exercise in and of themselves.

Thanksgiving Place Setting

by RENÉE DeBLOIS

Turkey Day is a great time for giving thanks in this personal touch for the table.

SUPPLIES

Tools

- [ ] spray bottle
- [ ] foam brush
- [ ] screw
- [ ] paper trimmer or cutting mat, craft knife, and ruler
- [ ] bone folder
- [ ] leaf punch
- [ ] ⅛-inch (3 mm) hole punch
- [ ] label maker with clear tape
- [ ] black marker
- [ ] universal hole punch

Materials

- [ ] walnut crystal stain
- [ ] manila folder
- [ ] butcher paper
- [ ] brown eyelets
- [ ] twine
- [ ] eyelet letters

INSTRUCTIONS

1. Mix the walnut crystal stain solution according to the directions and pour it into the spray bottle. Lay the manila folder on the butcher paper and spray it with the walnut stain solution. Use the foam brush to "distress" the paper by spreading the stain.

2. While the stain is wet, use a screw to draw shapes (such as swirls, starbursts, or botanic images) in the stain, being careful not to tear the folder. Spray on more stain to make the image darker. When it is dry, cut a piece of the folder to 7 inches tall x 4$\frac{7}{8}$ inches wide (17.8 x 12.4 cm). Use the bone folder to score and fold the card, creating a card base that is 3$\frac{1}{2}$ inches tall x 4$\frac{7}{8}$ inches wide (8.9 x 12.4 cm). (Card opens from the bottom).

3. Use the leaf punch to create 18 leaves with the remaining piece of the folder. Punch holes at the top of each leaf with the $\frac{1}{8}$-inch (3 mm) hole punch.

4. Punch two holes at the top left and right sides of the card base. Set brown eyelets into the holes. Thread the twine through one eyelet, tying a knot to hold it in place on the inside of the card.

5. Slip a few leaves onto the twine, then add an eyelet letter. Repeat this process until you reach the last letter. Feed the twine through the second hole and tie a second knot inside the card.

6. Print out "I'm thankful for" with the label maker with clear tape and attach the phrase to the bottom left edge of the card. Draw a line to the right of the phrase with the ruler and black marker. Use the universal hole punch and eyelet setter to spell "YOU" with the brown eyelet letters on the drawn line.

Black-Eyed Susan

by RENÉE DeBLOIS

Create a great big flower to say a great big thanks to someone you love.

SUPPLIES

Tools

- ☐ paper trimmer or cutting mat, craft knife, and ruler
- ☐ bone folder
- ☐ pencil
- ☐ universal hole punch
- ☐ eyelet setter
- ☐ 1½-inch (3.8 cm) circle punch
- ☐ wire cutters
- ☐ scissors

Materials

- ☐ orange cardstock
- ☐ large orange flower
- ☐ black fine-tipped marker
- ☐ white eyelets
- ☐ adhesive
- ☐ small alphabet letter stamps
- ☐ black ink

- ☐ 2-inch (5 cm) square photo
- ☐ small recycled plastic embellishment container
- ☐ small and large black brads
- ☐ mini black pom pom balls
- ☐ foam mounting tape
- ☐ super glue

INSTRUCTIONS

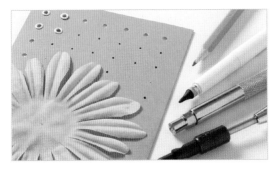

1. Cut the orange cardstock to 8 inches tall x 6 inches wide (20.3 x 15.2 cm). Score and fold the card with the bone folder to create a card base that is 4 inches tall x 6 inches wide (10.2 x 15.2 cm). (Card opens from the bottom.) Starting from the bottom edge of the card, mark a dot every ½ inch (1.3 cm) until you have marked a grid of 70 dots. Place the large orange flower on top of the card to determine which dots will be visible. Distinguish those dots with the black marker, and use the universal hole punch and eyelet setter to punch holes and set the white eyelets. Only 25 to 30 holes will be visible.

2. Glue the large orange flower to the card. Stamp the words "thanks for ma-king me laugh" between rows of eyelets using the alphabet stamps and black ink.

3. Trim your photo using the 1½-inch (3.8 cm) circle punch. Adhere the photo to the inside of the plastic embellishment container.

4. Cut the prongs from approximately 40 small and large black brads using wire cutters. Glue the brad tops onto the outside of the embellishment container cover with the super glue, starting at the center and radiating out. Fill in the holes with the small black pom pom balls.

5. Use foam mounting tape to fill the underside of the bottom of the embellishment container. Adhere this to the flower center. Screw on the container top to hide the photo.

Crocheted Flower

by CANDICE CRUZ

SUPPLIES

Tools

- ☐ paper trimmer or cutting mat, craft knife, and ruler
- ☐ bone folder
- ☐ scalloped square punch
- ☐ popsicle stick

Materials

- ☐ yellow cardstock
- ☐ patterned paper
- ☐ adhesive
- ☐ transparency paper, 2¾ inches (7 cm) square
- ☐ decorative line rub-ons
- ☐ mini glue dots
- ☐ crocheted flower
- ☐ "thanks" metal tag
- ☐ glitter glue

A little crocheted flower brings heartfelt thanks in this card.

INSTRUCTIONS

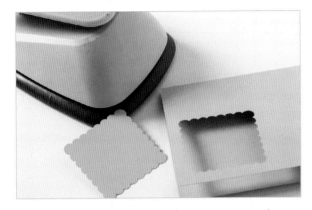

1. Cut the yellow cardstock to 5½ inches tall x 8½ inches wide (14 x 21.6 cm). Score and fold the card to a 5½ inches tall x 4¼ inches wide (14 x 10.8 cm) card base with the bone folder. (Card opens from the right). Punch a scalloped square window in the front of the card, about ½ inch (1.3 cm) from the bottom and right edges.

2. Cut the patterned paper to a 2½-inch (6.4 cm) square. Adhere it to the inside right side of the card, so that it shows through the window you created in the front of the card. Adhere the piece of transparency paper behind the window inside the left side of the card.

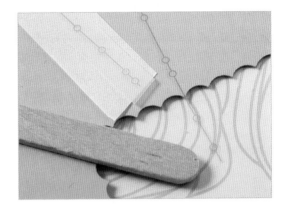

3. Use the popsicle stick to transfer the decorative line rub-on onto the front of the card. Continue the rub-on through the center of the window.

4. Use a mini glue dot to adhere the crocheted flower to the window on the front of the card. The flower will cover the place where the rub-ons meet in the center of the window. Apply a mini glue dot to the back of the metal tag and attach it to the front of the card, so that it's slipped slightly under the crocheted flower.

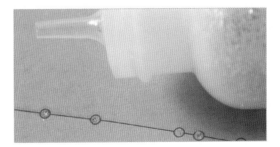

5. Add glitter glue to some of the little rub-on dots.

Puffy Pink Flowers

by CANDICE CRUZ

SUPPLIES

Tools

- ☐ paper trimmer or cutting mat, craft knife, and ruler
- ☐ scissors
- ☐ "merci bouquet" rubber stamp

Materials

- ☐ white cardstock
- ☐ patterned paper
- ☐ 15 inches (38.1 cm) of green and white ribbon, ⅛ inch (3 mm) wide
- ☐ three pink felt flowers
- ☐ mini glue dots
- ☐ crystal brads
- ☐ green stamp ink
- ☐ brown circle card, 5½-inch (14 cm) diameter

Cheerful pink flowers say "thank you" in this dainty card.

INSTRUCTIONS

1. Cut the white cardstock to ¾ inch tall x 3¼ inch wide (1.9 x 8.3 cm). Cut the patterned paper to 1 inch tall x 3½ inches wide (2.5 x 8.9 cm). Cut three pieces of green and white ribbon to 4-inch (10.2 cm), 3-inch (7.6 cm), and 2-inch (5 cm) lengths for the flower stems. Cut two additional pieces of green and white ribbon to 3-inch (7.6 cm) lengths.

2. Using a craft knife, pierce a small slit in the middle of each of the three felt flowers. Attach a crystal brad to the center of each flower.

3. Attach the "stems": Use a mini glue dot to adhere one end of each of the 4-inch (10.2 cm), 3-inch (7.6 cm), and 2-inch (5 cm) lengths of ribbon to the back of each flower. The 2-inch (5 cm) stem will be the leftmost flower; the 4-inch (10.2 cm) stem will be the center flower; and the 3-inch (7.6 cm) will be the rightmost flower. Tie the remaining 3-inch (7.6 cm) lengths of ribbon to the 2-inch (5 cm) and 4-inch (10.2) stems.

4. Adhere each flower to the front of the card using mini glue dots on the back of each ribbon stem and the flowers. Glue upward from the bottom of the ribbon stem to ensure the correct placement of the flowers.

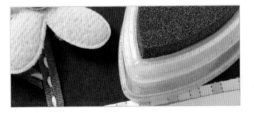

5. Stamp "merci bouquet" onto the white cardstock. When the ink is dry, ink the top, left, and bottom edges of the cardstock with the ink pad. Let the ink dry, then center and layer the cardstock onto the patterned paper. Adhere this paper to the bottom of the brown circle card so that it overlaps the third flower. Trim the message tag at an angle along the curve of the card.

Thanks a Latte!

by CANDICE CRUZ

Give someone a little caffeine boost along with your "thanks a latte" message.

SUPPLIES

Tools

- ☐ paper trimmer or cutting mat, craft knife, and ruler
- ☐ computer with word processing software and printer
- ☐ bone folder
- ☐ sewing machine
- ☐ tape

Materials

- ☐ brown cardstock
- ☐ black cardstock
- ☐ white cardstock
- ☐ adhesive
- ☐ glassine envelope
- ☐ black thread
- ☐ 3 inches (7.6 cm) of black satin ribbon, ¼ inch (6 mm) wide
- ☐ coffee shop gift card

thanks a latte!

the next one's on me!

1. Cut the brown cardstock to 7 inches tall x 10 inches wide (17.8 x 25.4 cm). Trim a second piece of brown cardstock to 1 inch tall x 3¾ inches wide (2.5 x 9.5 cm). Cut a piece of black cardstock to 6½ inches tall x 4½ inches wide (16.5 x 11.4 cm). Trim a piece of white cardstock to 6 inches tall x 4 inches wide (15.2 x 10.2 cm).

2. Using a computer with printer, print a 6-inch-tall x 4-inch-wide (15.2 x 10.2 cm) photo of a coffee cup with a black border onto white cardstock. Cut out the photo, leaving a ¼-inch (6 mm) white cardstock border around the edges. Using the bone folder, score and fold the larger piece of cut brown cardstock to create a 7-inch-tall x 5-inch-wide card base (17.8 x 12.7 cm). (Card opens from the right.) Center and adhere the photo piece to the front of the card.

3. Print the phrases "thanks a latte!" and "the next one's on me!" on the white cardstock, using a computer with word processing software. Cut "thanks a latte!" to ¾ inch tall x 3½ inches wide (1.9 x 8.9 cm). Cut "the next one's one me!" to 6 inches tall x 4 inches wide (15.2 x 10.2 cm), leaving about 1 inch (2.5 cm) of white space between "the next one's on me!" and the top edge of the cardstock.

5. Adhere the glassine envelope to the 6-inch-tall x 4-inch-wide (15.2 x 10.2 cm) white cardstock, leaving ½ inch (1.3 cm) between the bottom of the envelope and the bottom edge of the cardstock. Use a sewing machine and black thread to sew the three closed edges of the glassine envelope onto the white cardstock. Mount the white cardstock onto the black cardstock and then glue this to the inside of the card.

4. Layer the "thanks a latte!" phrase to the center of the 1-inch-tall x 3¾-inch-wide (2.5 x 9.5 cm) piece of brown cardstock. Attach the message to the front of the card.

6. Cut a 3-inch (7.6 cm) length of black satin ribbon. Fold it in half. Tape it to the back of the coffee shop gift card, leaving about ¼ inch (6 mm) sticking out on top so that it is easier to pull the card out of the pocket. Insert the gift card into the glassine envelope.

Holey Thanks

by **CANDICE CRUZ**

Give someone a "hole" lot of thanks with this circle window card.

SUPPLIES

Tools

- [ ] paper trimmer or cutting mat, craft knife, and ruler
- [ ] bone folder
- [ ] small circle dots stamp
- [ ] heat embossing tool
- [ ] circle cutting tool
- [ ] popsicle stick

Materials

- [ ] gray cardstock
- [ ] white cardstock
- [ ] adhesive
- [ ] watermark stamp pad

- [ ] purple embossing powder
- [ ] small alphabet rub-ons or stickers
- [ ] 22 inches (55 cm) of black satin ribbon, ¼ inch (6 mm) wide

INSTRUCTIONS

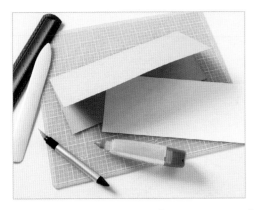

1. Cut the gray cardstock to 8½ inches tall x 9½ inches wide (21.6 x 24.1 cm). Score and fold with the bone folder to form a 4¼-inch-tall x 9½-inch-wide (10.8 x 24.1 cm) card base. Trim the white cardstock to 4 inches tall x 9¼ inches wide (10.2 x 23.5 cm) and adhere it to the inside of the card.

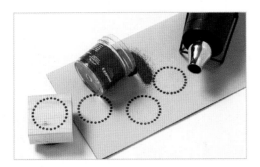

2. Open the card and lay it flat on the table. Using the watermark stamp pad and circle dots stamp, stamp the first of six circles towards the bottom left edge of the card. Sprinkle the embossing powder onto the image. Shake off the excess powder. Repeat this process for the remaining five circles. Use a heat embossing tool to set the embossing powder. Set the card aside to dry.

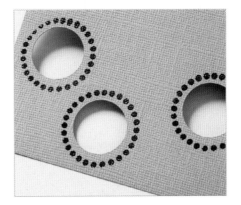

3. Once the embossing powder has dried, use a circle cutting tool to cut circles about 1 inch (2.5 cm) in diameter out of the center of each stamped circle.

4. Close the card and use the popsicle stick to transfer the rub-ons to the center of each circle to spell out "thanks." Tie a piece of the black ribbon across the top of the card and secure it with a double knot.

If Anyone Deserves Thanks

by CANDICE CRUZ

SUPPLIES

Tools

- [ ] paper trimmer or cutting mat, craft knife, and ruler
- [ ] bone folder
- [ ] flourish stamp
- [ ] heat embossing tool
- [ ] computer with word processing software and printer
- [ ] finger pointing right stamp
- [ ] corner rounder
- [ ] ribbon punch
- [ ] scissors
- [ ] pencil

Materials

- [ ] gray cardstock
- [ ] white rectangle cardstock with scalloped edge
- [ ] pink ink
- [ ] embossing powder
- [ ] adhesive
- [ ] black ink
- [ ] black cardstock
- [ ] 16 inches (40.6 cm) of black satin ribbon, ¼ inch (6 mm) wide
- [ ] thick alphabet stickers
- [ ] seven jewel stickers

Make it a point to say "thanks" with this fun card.

INSTRUCTIONS

1. Cut the gray cardstock to 11 inches tall x 5½ inches wide (27.9 x 14 cm). Score and fold the cardstock with the bone folder to create a 5½-inch (14 cm) square card base. (The card opens from the bottom.) Trim the scalloped cardstock to 5½ inches tall x 3¼ inches wide (14 x 8.3 cm).

2. Stamp the flourish image onto the white scalloped cardstock with pink ink. Apply embossing powder, using the heat embossing tool to set powder. Adhere the scalloped cardstock to the front of the card base, aligning left.

3. Using a computer with word processing software, print "If anyone deserves thanks it's" onto white cardstock. Cut the message to 1½ inches tall x 4 inches wide (3.8 x 10.2 cm), leaving white space around the phrase. Stamp the pointing finger image onto the rectangle with the black ink. Leave a ¼-inch (6 mm) margin to the left side of the image. Cut a piece of black cardstock to 1¾ inches tall x 4¼ inches wide (4.4 x 10.8 cm). Use the corner rounder to round the corners of the white and black pieces.

4. Use a ribbon punch to create a double slit to the left and right sides of the white cardstock piece. Thread the black satin ribbon through the slit on the right side and then up through the slot on left side.

5. Adhere alphabet stickers to spell "you!" Attach six jewel stickers underneath the stamped finger image and one on the period of the exclamation point.

6. Center and adhere the white rectangle to the black rectangle. Apply adhesive to the back of the black rectangle and adhere it to the bottom right of the card base. Wrap the ribbon around the card base and tie in a double knot on the front of the card. Trim off any excess ribbon.

Domo Arigato

by KELLY PURKEY

SUPPLIES

Tools

- ☐ paper trimmer or cutting mat, craft knife, and ruler
- ☐ bone folder
- ☐ popsicle stick
- ☐ scissors

Materials

- ☐ white cardstock
- ☐ two different kinds of patterned paper
- ☐ caramel cardstock
- ☐ adhesive
- ☐ robot stamp
- ☐ black ink
- ☐ transparency sheet
- ☐ silver and green metallic markers
- ☐ black rub-ons to spell "domo arigato mr. roboto"
- ☐ four brads
- ☐ pop-up glue dots

Have fun giving thanks with this adorable little robot.

INSTRUCTIONS

1. Cut the white cardstock to 5 inches tall x 8½ inches wide (12.7 x 21.6 cm). Trim one kind of patterned paper to 5 inches tall x 4¼ inches wide (12.7 x 10.8 cm). Cut the caramel cardstock to 4¾ inches tall x 3¼ inches wide (12.1 x 8.3 cm). Trim the second kind of patterned paper to 4½ inches tall x 3 inches wide (11.4 x 7.6 cm).

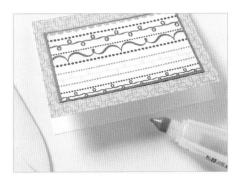

2. Score and fold the white cardstock with the bone folder to form a card base that is 5 inches tall x 4¼ inches wide (12.7 x 10.8 cm). (Card opens from the right). Adhere the first kind of patterned paper to the card base. Layer and adhere the caramel cardstock onto the card base. Adhere the second kind of patterned paper to the top of the caramel cardstock.

3. Stamp the robot onto the transparency. Trim the image to 4½ inches tall x 3¼ inches wide (11.4 x 8.3 cm). Flip the transparency over and color the robot with the silver and green markers. Use the popsicle stick to transfer rub-ons spelling "domo arigato mr. roboto" to the front of the transparency underneath the robot.

4. Attach a brad to each corner of the transparency. Use pop-up glue dots to adhere the transparency to the front of the card.

Thank You Tag

by KELLY PURKEY

SUPPLIES

Tools

- [ ] paper trimmer or cutting mat, craft knife, and ruler
- [ ] bone folder
- [ ] tag stamp
- [ ] wave decorative-edged scissors
- [ ] scissors
- [ ] sewing needle

Materials

- [ ] orange cardstock
- [ ] hot pink cardstock
- [ ] adhesive
- [ ] flower patterned paper
- [ ] orange ink
- [ ] white cardstock
- [ ] blue ink
- [ ] "thank you" stamp
- [ ] pink ink
- [ ] flower stamp
- [ ] 2 inches (5 cm) of green polka dot ribbon, ³⁄₈ inch (9.5 mm) wide
- [ ] pop-up glue dots
- [ ] pink button
- [ ] embroidery floss

Layer a little tag onto a regular card for a shabby chic look.

INSTRUCTIONS

1. Cut the orange cardstock to 5 inches tall x 8½ inches wide (12.7 x 12.6 cm). Cut a 3⅛-inch (7.9 cm) square piece of hot pink cardstock. Cut 2⅞-inch (7.3 cm) square piece of flower patterned paper. Score and fold the orange cardstock with the bone folder to create a 5-inch-tall x 4¼-inch-wide (12.7 x 10.8 cm) card base. Center and adhere the flower patterned paper square to the hot pink square. Attach this matted piece to the front of the card.

3. Fold the ribbon in half. Adhere it with a glue dot to the bottom of the button. Hand-sew the button to the right edge of the tag. Adhere the finished tag to the front of the card using pop-up glue dots.

2. Using orange ink, stamp the tag image onto white cardstock. Use the blue ink to stamp "thank you" and the pink ink to stamp the flower inside the tag shape. Use the wave decorative-edged scissors to cut the tag out.

Many Languages

by KELLY PURKEY

SUPPLIES

Tools

☐ paper trimmer or cutting mat, craft knife, and ruler

☐ bone folder

☐ scissors

☐ 2-inch (5 cm) circle punch

☐ 1½-inch (3.8 cm) circle punch

☐ popsicle stick

Materials

☐ dots patterned paper

☐ red paper

☐ blue paper

☐ green paper

☐ orange paper

☐ white cardstock

☐ rub-on letters

☐ five quote bubble chipboard pieces

☐ pop-up glue dots

☐ silver brads

This card shows how universal the phrase "thank you" really is.

INSTRUCTIONS

1. Cut the piece of patterned paper to 6 inches tall by 12 inches wide (15.2 X 30.4 cm) square. Fold it in half with the bone folder to create a 6-inch (15.2 cm) square card base (opens from the right). Punch one 2-inch (5 cm) circle from each of the red, blue, green, and orange papers. Adhere circles to the front of the card.

3. Adhere circles and quote bubbles to the front of the card with pop-up glue dots. Add silver brads onto the solid colored circles.

2. Punch five 1½-inch (3.8 cm) circles from the white cardstock. Use the popsicle stick to transfer rub-ons to write "merci," "gracias," "grazie," "thank you," and "dank u" on each of the five quote bubbles. Adhere one quote bubble onto each of the white circles.

Thank U

by KELLY PURKEY

Sometimes a small tag card is all you need to say thank you in a big way.

SUPPLIES

Tools

- ☐ paper trimmer or cutting mat, craft knife, and ruler
- ☐ sewing needle
- ☐ scissors
- ☐ ¼-inch (6 mm) hole punch

Materials

- ☐ silver paper
- ☐ adhesive
- ☐ black library pocket and tag insert
- ☐ patterned paper
- ☐ small alphabet stickers
- ☐ three flat-backed rhinestones

- ☐ large letter "u" embellishment
- ☐ mini glue dots
- ☐ embroidery floss
- ☐ pearl-ended hatpin
- ☐ 4 inches (10.2 cm) of red ribbon, ⅞ inch (2.2 cm) wide
- ☐ white marker

INSTRUCTIONS

1. Cut a ¼-inch tall x 4½-inch wide (6 mm x 11.4 cm) piece of silver paper. Adhere it ⅛ inch (3 mm) from the bottom of the library pocket. Cut a 1-inch-tall x 4½-inch-wide (2.5 x 11.4 cm) piece of the patterned paper. Adhere it directly above the silver strip of paper.

2. Use stickers to spell "thank" above the silver strip. Place three rhinestones to the left of the "thank."

3. Adhere the large letter "u" embellishment with glue dots to the right side of "thank." Hand stitch with the embroidery floss around a "leg" of the letter "u." Stick the pin through the thread.

4. Punch two holes through the top of the library card. Loop the red ribbon through the holes and tie it in a knot. Write a message on the tag with a white marker.

Slow to Thank

by WENDY WHITE

SUPPLIES

Tools

☐ paper trimmer (optional)

☐ cutting mat, craft knife, and ruler

☐ bone folder

☐ computer with word processing software and printer

Materials

☐ tree design paper

☐ light green cardstock

☐ frog sticker

☐ green accordion-fold cardstock

☐ adhesive

☐ turtle sticker

I know it's been a while

A belated thanks is better than no thanks at all when you send this silly card.

INSTRUCTIONS

1. Cut the tree design paper to 9 inches tall x 8 inches wide (22.9 x 20.3 cm), making sure the tree design will show on the front of the card. Score and fold the paper with the bone folder to create a card base measuring 9 inches tall x 4 inches wide (22.9 x 10.2 cm).

TIP: Card opens from the right.

2. Using a computer with word processing software, set page dimensions to 4¾ inches tall x 12 inches wide (12.1 x 30.4 cm). Create word art out of the word "really." Make one "really" that bends like the top of a circle and a second that bends like the bottom of a circle. Create one of each and copy and paste them along the page, moving them around to create a long row of curved up and down "really"s. Print the image onto light green cardstock and trim to 4¾ inches tall x 12 inches wide (12.1 x 30.4 cm), keeping about a 1-inch (2.5 cm) border below your text.

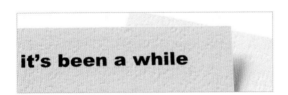

3. Using a computer with word processing software, print the phrases "I know it's been a while," "But I really . . . ," and "wanted to thank you" onto light green cardstock. Create text boxes so there will be enough room around your phrases to cut to the right size. Trim "I know it's been a while" to 1 inch tall x 4 inches wide (2.5 x 10.2 cm). Cut "But I really . . ." to 4¾ inches tall x 3 inches wide (12 x 7.6 cm). Trim "wanted to thank you" to 6 inches (15.2 cm) square.

4. Tape the "wanted to thank you" piece to the end of the "really, really, really" piece. Using a cutting mat and knife, cut a wavy border along the top. The "wanted to thank you" piece should be taller than the rest. Add a frog sticker below "wanted to thank you."

5. Layer and adhere the "really, really, really" piece on top of the accordion folded cardstock, lining up the bottom edges. Use the bone folder to score along the accordion's fold lines.

6. Score a fold 1½ inches (3.8 cm) from the left of the accordion-fold piece. Adhere this flap to the inside right of the card base, checking placement before attaching by folding up the accordion and closing the card to ensure it hides completely inside. Adhere "But I really . . ." to the inside of the card, hiding where the accordion fold meets the card base.

7. Adhere the "I know it's been a while" piece to the front of the card, approximately 1½ inches (3.8 cm) down from the top. Add the turtle sticker.

Big Thanks

by WENDY WHITE

Get your sentiment across in a big way with this fun, jumbo-letter thank you note.

INSTRUCTIONS

1. Cut the orange cardstock pieces as follows: Cut the first piece to 6 inches tall x 12 inches wide (15.2 x 30.4 cm) to form your card base. Trim another piece to 2 inches tall x 4 inches wide (5 x 10.2 cm) for the tag on the front of the card. Cut a third piece to 6 inches tall x 4 inches wide (15.2 x 10.2 cm) for the folded cardstock on which you will attach the "THANKS" inside.

   Cut two polka dot patterned paper pieces as follows: Trim one piece to 5½ inches (14 cm) square for the front of the card. Cut a second piece to 6 inches (15.2 cm) square for the inside right of the card. Cut one green cardstock piece to 1½ inches tall x 3½ inches wide (3.8 x 8.9 cm) to layer onto the orange tag on front of the card. Score the 6-inch-tall x 12-inch-wide (15.2 x 30.4 cm) orange cardstock with the bone folder to create the card base (opens from the right). Center and adhere the 5½-inch (14 cm) square polka dot paper to the front of the card. Adhere the to 6-inch (15.2 cm) square polka dot paper to the inside right of the card.

2. Using a computer with word processing software, create a document measuring 8½ inches x 21½ inches (21.6 x 54.6 cm). Change the page margins to "none" and the document orientation to horizontal. Type the word "THANKS" so the letters are 5½ inches (14 cm) tall and stretch the word to fit the length of the paper, about 20½ inches (52.1 cm). Flip the word so it appears in reverse. Print the image onto the blue accordion fold cardstock. Lay the printed cardstock on a mat and trim the word out using a knife and ruler, leaving ¼-inch (6 mm) connecting strips of cardstock between each letter at the top and bottom. Outline with your white and black pens to accent the word.

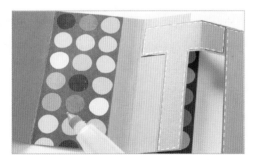

3. Use the bone folder to score the 6-inch-tall x 4-inch-wide (15.2 x 10.2 cm) piece of orange cardstock to create a folded piece 6 inches tall x 2 inches wide (15.2 x 5 cm). Adhere the "T" of the "THANKS" to the inner right side of the folded orange cardstock. Center and adhere the left side of the folded orange cardstock to the inside right of the 6-inch (15.2 cm) square card. Before gluing anything down, check your placement by folding up the word "THANKS" to ensure it will hide inside the card.

4. Assemble the tag for the front of the card: Center and adhere the 1½-inch-tall x 3½-inch-wide (3.8 x 8.9 cm) green cardstock onto the 2-inch-tall x 4-inch-wide (5 x 10.2 cm) orange cardstock. Use the popsicle stick to attach the rub-on "a big THANKS goes out to you" to the center of the tag. Use pop-up glue dots to adhere the tag to the front of the card about three-fourths of the way down and about ¼ inch (6 mm) from the right edge of the card. Use a double layer of pop-up glue dots to adhere the chipboard arrow to the left of the tag.

Black and Blue Medallion

by WENDY WHITE

SUPPLIES

Tools

- ☐ paper trimmer or cutting mat, craft knife, and ruler
- ☐ bone folder
- ☐ computer with word processing software and printer
- ☐ 2½-inch (6.4 cm) scalloped circle punch
- ☐ sewing machine

Materials

- ☐ green cardstock
- ☐ beige cardstock
- ☐ blue and white patterned paper
- ☐ white cardstock
- ☐ adhesive
- ☐ beige thread

Say it over and over again in this blue ribbon of a card.

INSTRUCTIONS

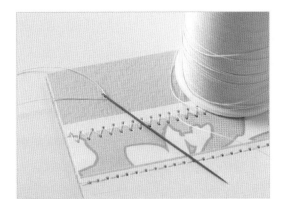

1. Cut the green cardstock to 6 inches tall x 12 inches wide (15.2 x 30.4 cm). Trim a piece of beige cardstock to $4\frac{3}{8}$ inches tall x 6 inches wide (11.1 x 15.2 cm). Trim a second piece of beige cardstock to $2\frac{3}{4}$ inches tall x 6 inches wide (7 x 15.2 cm). Cut a piece of green cardstock to $2\frac{7}{8}$ inches tall x 6 inches wide (7.3 x 15.2 cm). Trim another piece of green cardstock to $5\frac{7}{8}$ inches (14.9 cm) square. Trim the blue and white patterned paper to 4 inches tall x 6 inches wide (10.2 x 15.2 cm). Score the 6-inch-tall x 12-inch-wide (15.2 x 30.4 cm) green cardstock with the bone folder to create a 6-inch (15.2 cm) square card base.

3. Adhere the small piece of beige cardstock to the smaller piece of green cardstock. There will be a very narrow mat on both sides. Adhere the blue and white patterned paper to the larger piece of beige cardstock. Center and attach the smaller matted beige and green cardstock onto the larger matted piece. Sew two lines along the beige part of the smaller matted piece. Sew a zigzag stitch where the patterned paper meets the beige cardstock. Trim the threads and adhere the entire stitched piece to the front of the card base.

2. Use a computer with word processing software to create a $2\frac{3}{4}$-inch (7 cm) diameter black circle. Layer a $2\frac{1}{4}$-inch (5.7 cm) diameter light blue circle with a white outline over it. Add and center a text box with white letters spelling "Thank You." Print the medallion onto white cardstock. Use the scalloped circle punch to cut the image out of cardstock.

4. Adhere the black and blue medallion onto the right side of the card, vertically centered on the beige area. Adhere the $5\frac{7}{8}$-inch (14.9 cm) square piece of green cardstock to the inside of the card.

TIP: Print a personal message on the green cardstock before you adhere it to the card, if desired.

Expressions of Thanks

GREETINGS

Choosing a greeting or sentiment for your card is an important first step to setting the right tone. First decide what type of card style you want: classic, modern, humorous, cute, intricate, or otherwise. Your greeting and message will often dictate the types of materials you use, the layout of your card, images to incorporate, and any unique features or embellishments. Greetings and sentiments can be handmade using a computer and printer. Or they can be created with rubber stamps and ink. You can also find stickers, rub-ons, and other embellishments to do the trick for you.

QUOTES

There's nothing wrong with stealing the words from someone else's mouth if they fit what you're trying to say. Quotes can simply and succinctly convey your feelings to your loved ones. We offer some suggestions on the following four pages. You can also try these helpful websites for quotes: www.coolquotes.com and www.worldofquotes.com.

HANDWRITING

In today's technology-driven world, there's nothing sexier and more intimate than personal handwriting. Take the time to hand write your message for a truly personal approach. If you don't like the look of your own handwriting, incorporate just a bit of it into your card. You can sign your name yourself or write your loved one's name or initials. Use a computer, rubber stamps, or rub-ons for the rest of your text.

POSTAL REGULATIONS

Cards of unique shapes, sizes, and weights may require additional postage to mail. Always check with your local post office to ensure your handmade card arrives at your loved one's destination. Also, try not to mail your card on days when bad weather is expected, to avoid smudging and water damage.

Let us be grateful to people who make us happy; they are the charming gardeners who make our souls blossom.
–Marcel Proust

I would thank you from the bottom of my heart, but for you, my heart has no bottom.

I can no other answer make, but, thanks and thanks.
–William Shakespeare

Not what we give, but what we share, for the gift without the giver is bare.
–James Russell Lowell

If the only prayer you ever
say in your entire life is
thank you, it will be enough.
−Meister Eckhart

The smallest act of kindness is worth
more than the grandest intention.
−Oscar Wilde

Thank you for the helping hand and the open heart.

I feel a very unusual sensation−if it is not
indigestion, I think it must be gratitude.
−Benjamin Disraeli

Thanks!
I appreciate you!

How beautiful a day can be
when kindness touches it!
—George Elliston

Unselfish and noble actions
are the most radiant pages
in the biography of souls.
—David Thomas

Thanks...
not just for what you did,
but for being you!

Gratitude is the
sign of noble souls.
—Aesop

Anyone can be a dad—
but it takes a man to be a father.
Thank you for being such a wonderful father!

How do you mail a hug?
Thank you so much!

At times our own light goes out and is rekindled by a spark from another person. Each of us has cause to think with deep gratitude of those who have lighted the flame within us.
–Albert Schweitzer

I would maintain that thanks are the highest form of thought, and that gratitude is happiness doubled by wonder.
–Gilbert Keith Chesterton

God invented mothers because he couldn't be everywhere.
Thank you for being such a wonderful mother!

Contributors

CANDICE CRUZ

Candice Cruz has a passion for celebrating memories through photography and scrapbooking. Her other hobbies include card making, cooking, knitting, and jewelry making. Her layouts and greeting cards have been published in several magazines and books. To see her work, visit www.shortcakescraps.com. Candice lives in Massachusetts.

KIM KESTI

Kim Kesti is addicted to paper crafting. Since she was a little girl, Kim has been playing with paper and glue, and today she enjoys scrapbooking and card making. She likes to use her hobby to bring a little joy to those around her. Kim lives in Arizona.

RENÉE DeBLOIS

Crafty since her Girl Scout years, Renée DeBlois first focused on scrapbooking, cross-stitching, rubber stamping, and card making. More recently, she has taken to knitting, otherwise known as collecting yarn. Renée is drawn to geometric modern art and anything black and white. As a novice fiction writer, she has started using scrapbooking and journaling as a way to develop characters and ideas. She teaches paper crafting classes and has had cards published in *Cards* and *Paper Crafts* magazines. Renée lives in Massachusetts.

KELLY PURKEY

Working as a graphic designer by day, Kelly Purkey loves to come home and keep on creating. Kelly has been scrapbooking for seven years and has a bookcase full of albums she cherishes. She enjoys finding inspiration in everyday objects and is always on the lookout for new ideas. Kelly lives in Illinois.

WENDY WHITE

Wendy White owns and operates Scrapsupply, an online scrapbook store. Wendy has been making cards for five years and enjoys discovering new techniques and products through her work as a store owner. Wendy has an online gallery of her cards and other creations at www.scrapsupply.com. She is a happily married mother of three children.

Acknowledgments

The authors would like to thank all the friends they worked alongside at Spark Craft Studios, whose talent and enthusiasm continue to inspire us; our husbands and families, whose love and support allows us to do work that is meaningful and fun; and all of our readers, whose continuing interest in crafting makes books like *Thank You Notes* possible.

About the Authors

JAN STEPHENSON KELLY and AMY APPLEYARD co-founded Spark Craft Studios, Inc., a stylish, modern spin on the traditional craft store, in 2005. Their unique concept combined a craft supply retail store with a lounge-like studio space and catered to community-oriented crafters in Cambridge, Massachusetts, until 2008. Spark Craft Studios helped hundreds of people explore their creativity, integrate crafts into their lives, and even start their own craft businesses. Jan and Amy have won awards for innovative retailing, and been featured in *Time*, *Business Week* Online, *The Boston Globe*, DailyCandy, *Lucky* magazine, and more, for their work with Spark. Before founding Spark, Jan worked in marketing and fundraising for prominent nonprofit organizations. Amy managed her own theatrical lighting design company based in New York, and worked with theater and opera companies all over the United States. Jan has a B.A. in journalism from Ithaca College, and an M.B.A. from Boston University. Amy holds a B.A. in theatre arts from Virginia Tech and an M.B.A. from Boston University. Jan and Amy are also co-editors of *Love Notes: 40 Exquisite Handmade Cards to Express Your Love*.

Resources

It's all on www.larkbooks.com

Can't find the materials you need to create a project? Search our database for craft suppliers & sources for hard-to-find materials.

Got an idea for a book? Read our book proposal guidelines and contact us.

Want to show off your work? Browse current calls for entries.

Want to know what new and exciting books we're working on? Sign up for our free e-newsletter.

Feeling crafty? Find free, downloadable project directions on the site.

Interested in learning more about the authors, designers & editors who create Lark books?

Index